Costumed Teddy Bears

14 Patterns for Bears in Body Suits

❧Creative Crafters❧

Costumed Teddy Bears
14 Patterns for Bears in Body Suits

Celia Baham

Portfolio Press

ACKNOWLEDGEMENTS

I would like to thank my mother for teaching me about fabrics and how to use a sewing machine. I also want to thank my greatest fan, my husband, whom I love dearly for his patience for the cluttered house during creative times, and for his unfailing support in my quest for creativity. Thanks go to my family and friends for allowing me to use their names for my creations. Chris Revi was my mentor and supporter — I will always cherish our friendship. To my children, Jeff Baham and Jeanine Bailey, thanks for giving me the time and helpful feedback on design efforts. Thank you Betty Unger for taking me to the first teddy bear convention in San Jose, California. Thank you Neysa Phillippi for always challenging me, pushing my limits in designing. And I want to thank you, the collector and artist for enjoying my bears and taking my classes. One of my greatest joys is teaching and developing new artists!

First edition/First printing

To purchase additional copies of this book, please contact:
Portfolio Press, 130 Wineow Street, Cumberland, MD 21502
877-737-1200

Library of Congress Control Number 2001-135273
ISBN 0-942620-54-2

Project Editor: Krystyna Poray Goddu
Design and Production: Tammy S. Blank
Computer work: Steve Baham, Jeff Baham
Photographs: Steve and Celia Baham
Author's portrait photo: Lifetouch Church Directories
Cover design by John Vanden-Heuvel Design

Printed and bound in Korea

Contents

Santa

Ming Panda

Painted-Face Jester

Jasmine the Ballerina

Tina

Santa's Helper

Santa With Bag

Clown-Face Jester

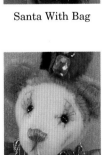

Roosevelt

Pajama Bear

Chef Chris

Punky

Mr. & Mrs. Farmer

BASIC DIRECTIONS

A Word About Fabrics

Mohair is the traditional fabric for teddy bears, and is the fabric of choice for the bears in this book. Synthetic fur plush, however, can look just as good and is less expensive. Some patterns combine mohair with upholstery, knit or other types of fabric that may have the capacity to stretch. When mixing the materials on one bear, some easing or pulling of the fabric may be necessary to make the paw pads fit the arm and leg pieces, since the mohair (and European plush) are woven and do not stretch. Let's define two important terms you will see in the instructions.

■ Pile is the furry side of the fabric. Pile comes in different lengths, thickness, and density, and can be straight, kinky, wavy, or sparse.

■ Nap is a characteristic of furry fabrics, and refers to the way the fur lies smoothly when you rub your hand lightly over it. Some types of mohair change nap direction every 18 inches, so check the direction every 18 inches or so to be sure the nap direction is right for the piece.

And remember: If you have any doubts about the fabric dye, wash the piece before dyeing it. It would be frustrating to spend hours working on a bear just to have the dye rub off on your clothes!

Making A Permanent Pattern

Always trace pattern pieces; never cut the pattern pieces out of the book. Use tracing paper, then cut the pieces out of the tracing paper and trace those onto light cardboard. The back of cereal boxes is an ideal weight for a sturdy pattern. If you prefer, you may trace the pattern pieces onto plastic sheets that quilters use to make templates. You can find these sheets in quilt shops. Whatever you use, be sure to mark all pattern pieces and include darts, joint placements, openings for stuffing, etc. Mark the center front of the foot pad (sole). If one pattern piece is used for both a right and left part, mark it "cut 2 (1 reverse)." It's also a good idea to include the name of the pattern and the number of the piece, for example, "2 of 7," to keep track of all the pieces of the pattern.

Laying Out The Pattern On The Fabric

Trace all of the pattern pieces onto the fabric. For pieces marked "cut 2 (1 reverse)" make sure to flip the pattern before tracing the second piece. Double check that the reversed pieces have both a right and a left side. Make sure that joint markings are on a right side and a left side. Place the pattern pieces as close together as possible on the fabric. Be sure that the nap lines up with the direction of the arrows on the patterns. Mark the backing with permanent ink pens. Use a very thin point for the miniatures and a medium point for larger bears. On dark fabric backings, use a seamstress white or yellow marking pencil. Be sure you have placed all of the pattern pieces on the fabric before you begin cutting, so you know that the pieces fit properly.

Cutting Patterns

Cut carefully along the outside edge of the pattern, using sharp scissors. Cut only the fur backing, not the pile. Place the scissors blade right up against the backing to avoid cutting into the pile. Save all the scraps to use for ears on another bear. Save even the little one-inch pieces for stuffing large bears; doing so adds weight to the bear and uses up every bit of that expensive fabric!

Sewing Pieces Together

Before you begin, read through the pattern instructions and look at the diagrams to get an idea of how the parts fit and are sewn together.

The patterns include a seam allowance of approximately 1/4 inch. To ensure an accurate fit, pin the pieces together before you start to sew. The head gusset tends to stretch, so pin or baste it in place before sewing to the side head. Similarly, baste the sole to the foot before machine sewing.

Use #16 or #18 sewing machine needles. If you are using gold, brown, beige, or any light-colored fabric, use beige thread for the small stitches. Clear nylon serger thread is good if the bear is to be stuffed with pellets. If a bear is made up of several colors, make sure to change the thread color to correspond with the fabric.

When sewing with fabrics that fray easily, use Fray Check on the seams before turning them inside out. This will also create a line you can follow when closing seams.

Attaching Ears

Attach the ears to the stuffed head with the "three-point-ear" technique. Use nylon thread for strength, as people often pick bears up by their ears. Secure the ears especially well at the corners.

Point A and point B indicate where the outside corners of the ear attach to the head. Point C indicates where the center attaches. Once you have decided where to attach the ear, knot the thread (point A). Thread the ear on the needle and push the needle through the head from just behind the knot at A to point B. Sew through the ear at point B and pull the ear to the head. Push the needle through the head from point B to point C.

Sew through the ear at point C and knot the thread on the inside of the ear. This method ensures that the knots are pulled to the inside of the ear, and won't be visible.

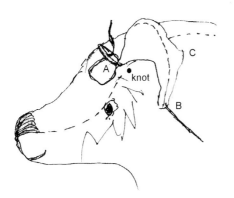 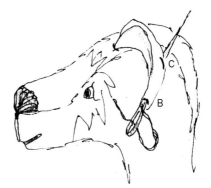

Attaching The Eyes

The most common types of eyes are glass and plastic safety eyes. Glass eyes have a straight wire or wire loop. If the eye has a straight wire, bend the wire into a loop and twist the ends of the wire tightly so the loop cannot pull loose. Plastic eyes have a shank with a hole through it. Eyes with loops are put on the bear after the head is stuffed.

Here's how to make sure the eyes are positioned evenly. Place a large-headed pin in each side of the head at the approximate position you plan to have each eye. Place a third pin in the center of the nose. Take a pipe cleaner and bend it about 1/2-inch around the pin at one eye location. Gently bend the other end of the pipe cleaner around the center nose pin. The two bends "measure" the distance from the nose to one eye. Carefully remove the pipe cleaner from the eye pin without unbending it and swing it over to the other eye pin. Adjust the position of the eye pin as needed, so that the distance from nose to eye pin is the same for both eyes. When you are satisfied with the position of the eyes, make an opening with an awl at each eye pin location.

Place thread through loop in eye piece and center the eye on the thread. Place both ends of thread through eye of needle and insert in opening made by awl. Come out at neck edge. Pull one thread out of needle and insert needle back into fabric and come out 1/8 of an inch away. This gives the knot something to hold it in place. Now make a knot and pull tight. Then go back into head (next to knot) with needle, with both ends of thread for about 2 inches, then come out and cut remaining ends of thread off (this secures the thread).

Safety eyes, on the other hand, are put on before the head is stuffed. If you are making a bear that may be played with by a child, safety eyes are the better choice. Safety eyes have a solid plastic shank onto which a safety disk is pushed to lock the eye firmly against the fabric.

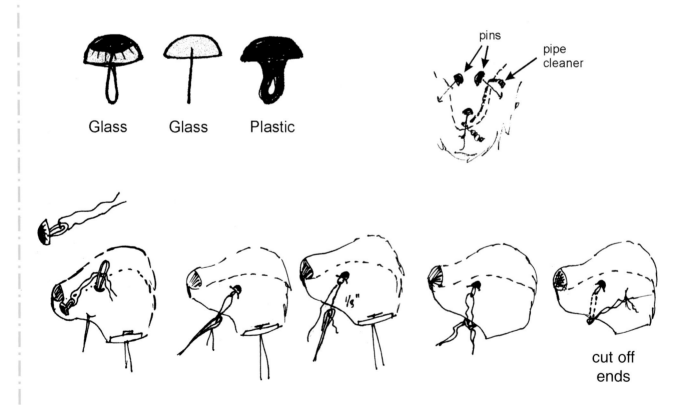

Glass   Glass   Plastic

pins   pipe cleaner

cut off ends

Stitching The Nose and Mouth

First, you must choose a nose style to fit the personality of the bear you are making. Here is one procedure I use for stitching the nose and mouth.

Begin by making a template from 100 percent wool felt. Then attach the template to the nose location on the head, and embroider over the template.

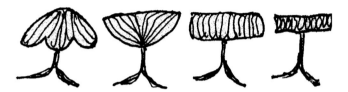

Embroider the nose with closely spaced stitches. Use pearl cotton sizes #3 and #5 to sew the nose and the mouth, too. Waxing the nose makes it shiny. If you decide you want this look, warm a small piece of beeswax to soften it, then rub it into the finished embroidered nose. Polish with a toothbrush.

To stitch the mouth, begin by attaching the thread to the head at the corner of the mouth. Knot the thread at point 1. Push the needle through the muzzle from point 2 to point 3, catching the thread as shown. Stitch the mouth to the head at point 3. If the mouth is curved, hold the curve in place by stitching additional points between points 1 and 3, and 2 and 3.

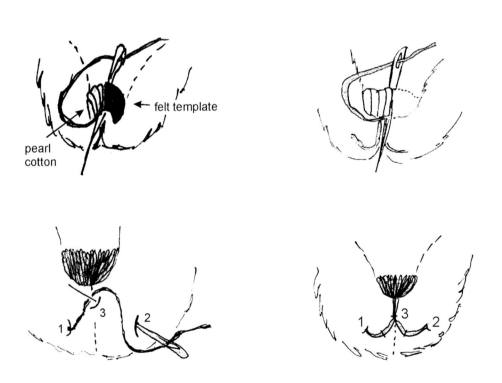

Joint Construction

A fully jointed bear has five joints: one that joins the head to the body and one for joining each of the two arms and two legs to the body. There are several methods of jointing. Two of the most common use cotter pins or nuts and bolts. T-cotter pins make suitable joints for smaller bears. Nuts and bolts are stronger, and should be used on larger bears to provide extra strength.

A "joint set" is made up of all of the materials required to assemble one joint: two disks, two fender washers and either a T-cotter pin or nut and bolt.

Attach the head first, as it is still easier to work with the small area around the neck. Insert the head joint cotter pin, fender washer and fiber disk into the head as you are stuffing and closing it. After the body is sewn, gather the neck opening, pull it closed and secure it with a knot. Insert the head joint cotter pin through the center of the gathered neck edge, and complete the joint with the remaining half of the joint set (fiber disk and fender washer) inside the body.

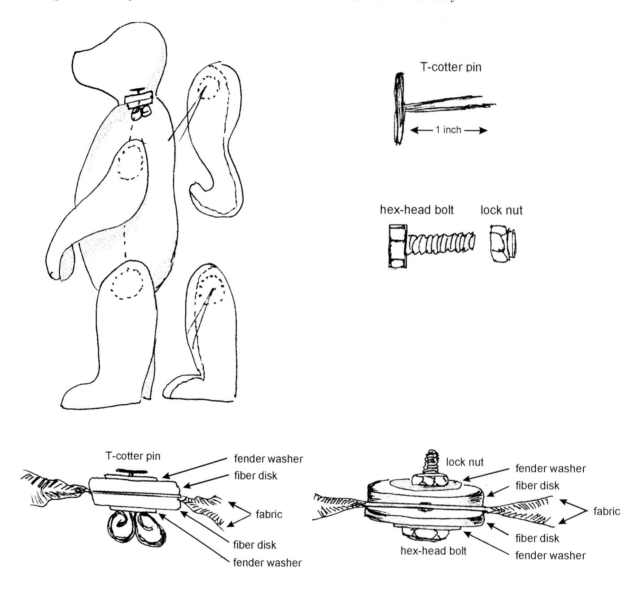

Attach the arms and legs before stuffing. Use an awl to make an opening on the arm and leg joint marks of the body. Then make joint openings in the arms and legs. Place a fender washer and fiber disk on a T-cotter pin (or bolt). Push the cotter pin through the arm joint hole from inside the arm into the joint hole in the body. Put another fiber disk and fender washer on the cotter pin inside the body.

Use needle-nose pliers to turn the arms of the cotter pin outward in a tight circle so that the arms press firmly against the fender washer. Cotter pins can also be turned tightly by using a commercial turner such as the EKLIND 7/32 No. 51614 cotter pin turner. Make the joints as tight as possible because they tend to loosen as the bear is stuffed.

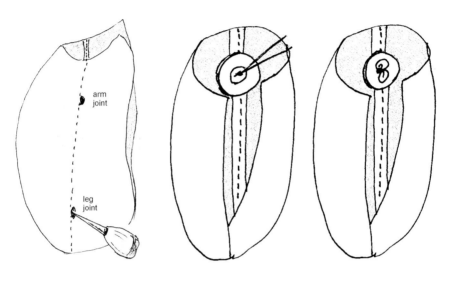

Stuffing

Turn the pieces of the bear (head, body, arms, legs) right side out. Stuff the head starting with the nose. Put small puffs (about one-inch diameter) of fiberfill into the tip of the nose, forcing them in until the nose is solid. If the bear is large enough, use a stuffing tool. Stuff the remainder of the head with larger pieces of fiberfill. When the head is filled to the desired hardness, insert cotter pin, fender washer and fiber disk (one half of a joint set) into the neck opening and gather closed tightly around the cotter pin.

Stuff the body with fiberfill. Pack the stuffing with a fiber stuffer to make the body firm. Stuff the legs and arms until solid and close. Close the body last, in case additional stuffing is required. When the stuffing is complete, close the seams with a ladder stitch.

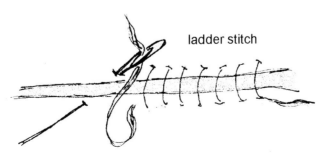

ladder stitch

Useful Hints

■ If you are unfamiliar with needle sculpting, try to design the pattern pieces exactly how you want them finished. For example, if you want eyes closer together, adjust the head gusset to be nearer the desired eye location.

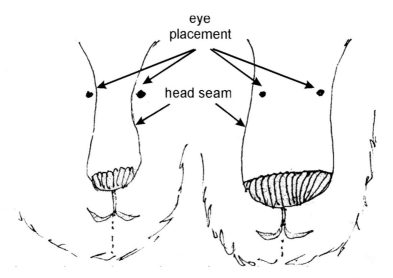

■ If you want turned-up shoes (like those the Santa's Helper wears), turn them up. Be bold, be creative!

■ When painting a bear's face (like that of the Painted-Face Jester), use acrylic paints that clean up with water. Use the dry-brush technique for better control of the color. If the paint is too wet, it will spread over the fabric.

■ When shaving a bear's muzzle (like that of the Santa or Roosevelt bears), first cut the fur close to the backing. Then shave the rest clean with a mustache trimmer. The Norelco Maverick t-3000 mustache trimmer has attachments for smaller or larger areas.

■ When using shot, pellets, or glass bead for stuffing, be sure to double-stitch the seams and mark the bear labels that these are "adult collectibles," and not meant for small children. Always use safety eyes and polyester fiberfill for bears that may be played with by children under ten years of age.

■ If you want to see how a design will look before cutting into expensive fabric, first make the pattern with paper towels. Scotch tape the pieces together to see if the design will work.

■ If you are using excelsior for stuffing, try to find the soft kind that comes from Germany. The type of excelsior found in gift baskets can be used, but is a little stiff. Work it over in your hands until it is soft enough to fit in the head. Excelsior is ideal for stuffing heads, because it makes the nose easier to sew.

■ Buy plastic pellets in bulk. General Polymer, a subsidiary of Ashland Chemical (408-370-1144), manufactures pellets.

■ Always comb the fur out of the seams. A metal dog comb works very nicely for combing out 1/4-inch seams. Use a Bunka brush for combing fur out of the seams on the right side.

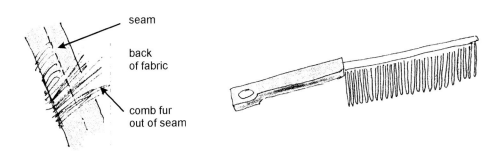

■ The most common type of bear joint is a 2½-inch diameter fiber disk. If the right size disk isn't available, make one yourself out of cardboard. Cut the cardboard to the required size, then build up a thick disk by gluing layers on top of each other with white fast-drying glue. Put them under a heavy object so they'll dry hard and flat. Three or four layers make a hard center. When the glue is dry, make a hole in the center of the disk with an awl. For added strength, add a small (1/2-inch diameter) metal washer to the outside of the fiber disks.

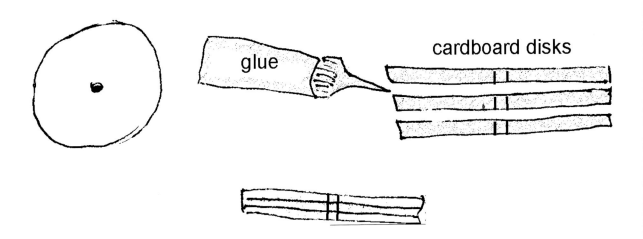

Tina

(Size: 9 inches; Difficulty Level: 1)

MATERIALS

- ☐ 1/4 yard of light gold mohair or wool, 1/2" pile
- ☐ One 9" x 9" light gold 100% wool felt for paws
- ☐ One each 10" and 12" crochet doilies for dress
- ☐ One pair of 6mm glass or plastic eyes
- ☐ Five 1" fiber disk joint sets for head, arms, and legs
- ☐ #5 black pearl cotton for nose and mouth
- ☐ Sewing-machine thread for seams, color to match fabric
- ☐ Polyester fiberfill for stuffing
- ☐ Nylon upholstery thread for attaching eyes and closing seams

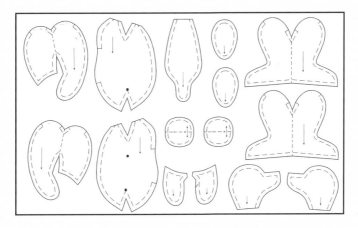

This diagram represents all of the pattern pieces required to complete this bear, laid out in the straight of the fabric. More than one piece of fabric may be required for laying out the pattern pieces.

INSTRUCTIONS

1

Sew side head from nose down to neck edge.

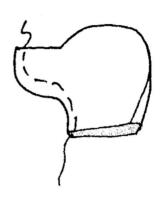

2

Sew other side head from nose down to neck edge.

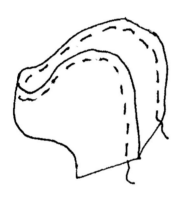

3

Fold ear and sew, cutting the center for turning.

cut and
leave open

4

Match seam lines and sew felt paw to arm for both right and left arms.

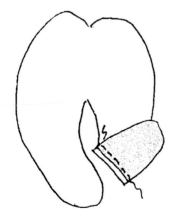

5

Fold arm and sew, leaving the top part open for stuffing.

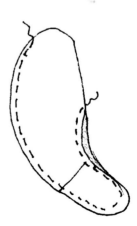

6

Fold leg in half and sew, leaving the top open for stuffing.

For both legs, baste the sole into the bottom of the leg, then machine-sew the sole to the leg.

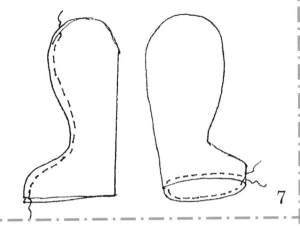

7

Sew two body pieces together, front and back, leaving the center back open for stuffing.

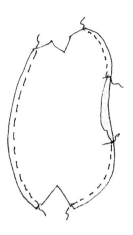

8

Sew darts in top and bottom of body. Refer to the Basic Directions to complete the head and attach the head, arms, and legs to the body. Stuff and close the open seams.

9

Tina's dress is made from a large and small doily. The larger doily forms the skirt and the smaller forms the bodice.

In the center of the smaller doily zig-zag a circle large enough to go around the head of the bear. Cut out the center of the doily inside the stitching.

10

Similarly zig-zag a circle in the center of the larger doily to go around the waist of the bear. Cut out the center of the doily inside the stitching.

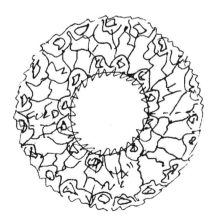

11

Place the skirt and bodice doilies on the body.

Hand-sew the bodice to the skirt at the waist in front and back. The sides are left open for the arms.

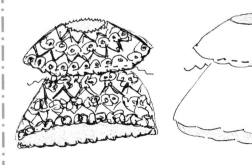

12

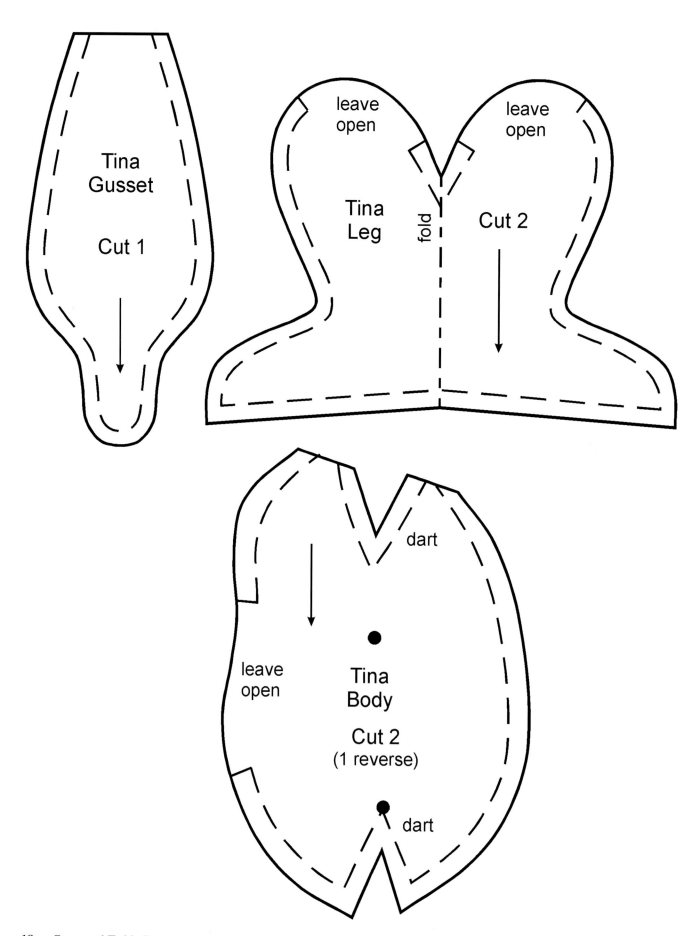

Tina
Gusset

Cut 1

leave
open

leave
open

Tina
Leg

fold

Cut 2

dart

leave
open

Tina
Body

Cut 2
(1 reverse)

dart

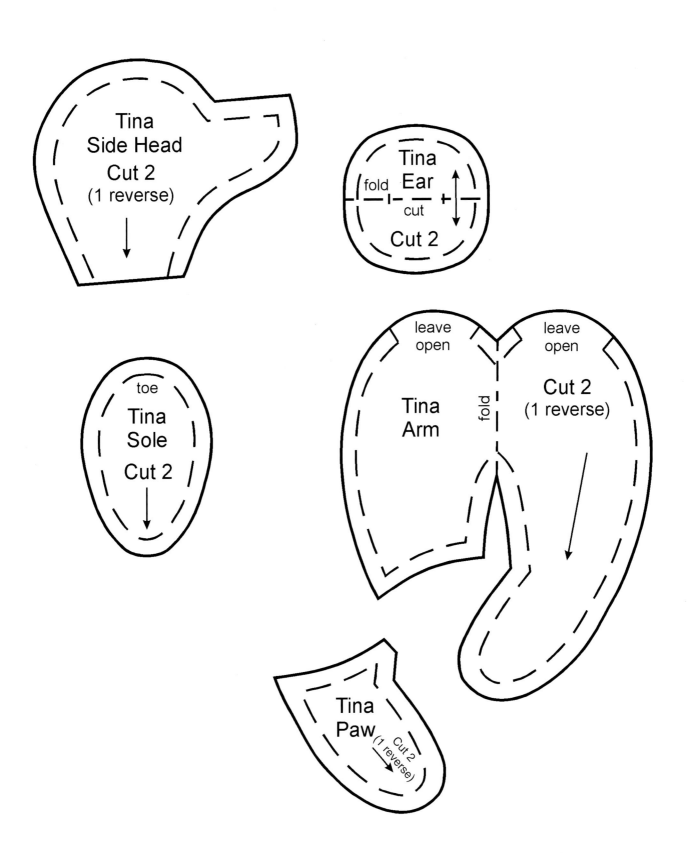

Tina
Side Head
Cut 2
(1 reverse)

Tina
Ear
fold
cut
Cut 2

toe
Tina
Sole
Cut 2

leave open
leave open
Tina
Arm
fold
Cut 2
(1 reverse)

Tina
Paw
Cut 2
(1 reverse)

Jasmine
the Ballerina

(Size: 11 inches; Difficulty Level: 2)

MATERIALS

- ☐ One piece 5" x 10" beige mohair, 1/8" pile, for arms, chest, ears, front of head
- ☐ One piece 7" x 8" light green mohair, 1/8" pile, for body
- ☐ One piece 8" x 12" white 1/8" mohair for legs
- ☐ One piece 3" x 3" blonde mohair, 1½" pile, for back of head
- ☐ One piece 2" x 4" beige 100% wool felt for paws
- ☐ One piece 2" x 4" black 100% wool felt for soles
- ☐ One piece 14" x 3½" netting for tutu
- ☐ One small tube of black acrylic paint for shoes
- ☐ One pair 4mm eyes, glass or plastic
- ☐ Small T-cotter pins for joints
- ☐ 20 balloon saucers for joints (3/4" thin plastic disks, available in party goods stores)
- ☐ #5 brown pearl cotton for nose
- ☐ Polyester fiberfill and plastic pellets
- ☐ Sewing-machine thread for seams, color to match fabrics
- ☐ Waxed thread for attaching eyes
- ☐ Nylon upholstery thread for closing seams

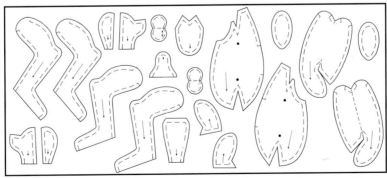

This diagram represents all of the pattern pieces required to complete this bear, laid out in the straight of the fabric. More than one piece of fabric may be required for laying out the pattern pieces.

INSTRUCTIONS

1

Sew two side heads to side head gusset. This forms the front half of the head.

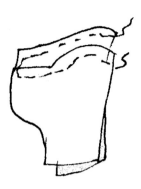

2

Sew side heads together from nose down to neck edge.

1/8" mohair

3

Sew back head to back head gusset. Sew front of head to back of head.

1" mohair

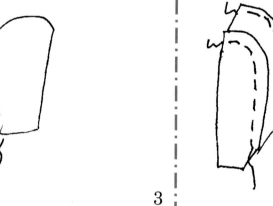

4

Sew center front body seam.

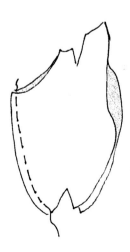

5

Sew chest piece into top front of body.

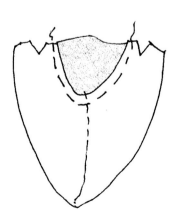

6

Sew darts at neck and at bottom of body. Sew back of body seam. Leave the center open for stuffing.

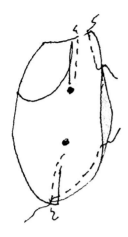

7

Sew paw to arm, fold arm and sew leaving top open for stuffing. Make both right and left arms.

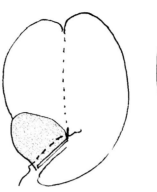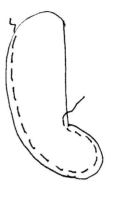

8

Sew two leg pieces together leaving the top open for stuffing. Make two legs. Sew one sole to each leg.

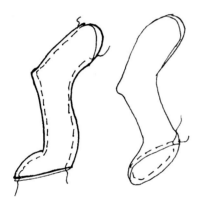

9

Refer to the Basic Directions to complete the head and attach the head, arms, and legs to the body. Stuff and close the open seams.

Cut a 14" by 3½" piece of netting for the tutu. Sew 1" satin ribbon or grosgrain ribbon to gathered netting.

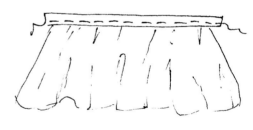

10

Gather netting around Jasmine's waist to check the fit and sew the side seam, leaving 1½" open from the top. Tie the ribbon in a bow.

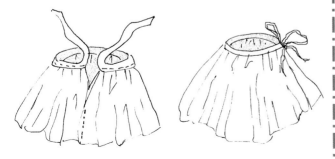

11

Shave the fur from the area of the foot where the "shoes" will be painted.

Paint shoes with 3 coats of black acrylic paint, letting each coat dry before applying the next.

For a shiny look, paint the shoes with a coat of finger-nail hardener.

12

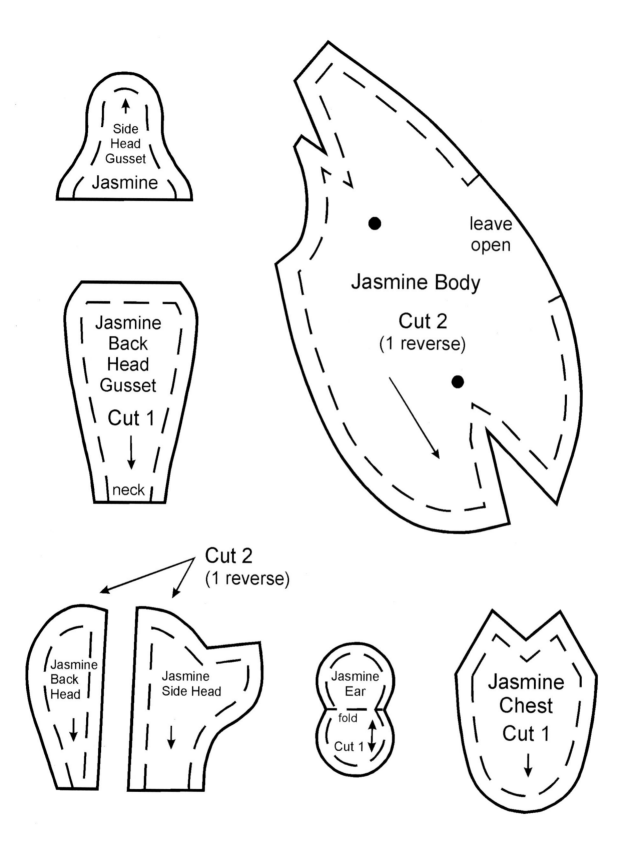

Side
Head
Gusset

Jasmine

Jasmine
Back
Head
Gusset

Cut 1

neck

leave
open

Jasmine Body

Cut 2
(1 reverse)

Cut 2
(1 reverse)

Jasmine
Back
Head

Jasmine
Side Head

Jasmine
Ear

fold

Cut 1

Jasmine
Chest

Cut 1

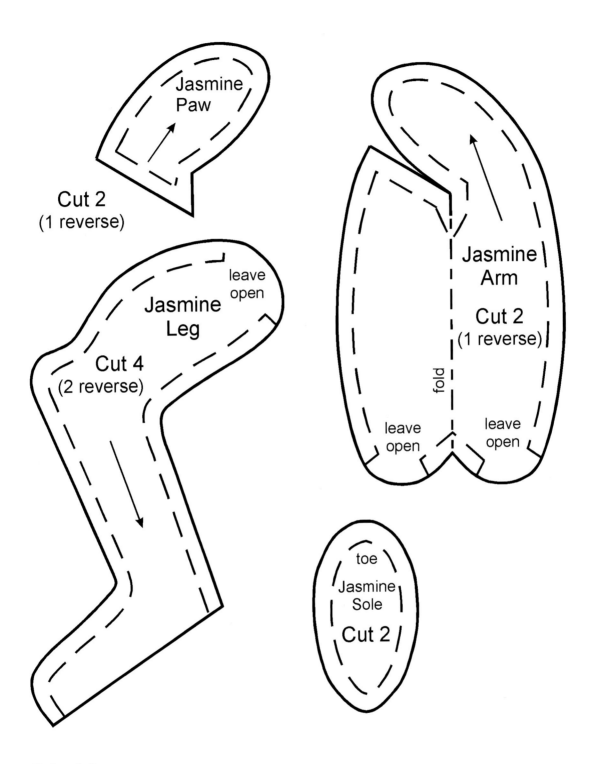

Jasmine Paw

Cut 2
(1 reverse)

Jasmine
Arm

Cut 2
(1 reverse)

fold

leave
open

leave
open

Jasmine
Leg

leave
open

Cut 4
(2 reverse)

toe

Jasmine
Sole

Cut 2

Beige felt: paw

Black felt: sole

Beige mohair: side head, side head gusset, ear, arm, leg, chest

Green mohair: body

Long yellow mohair: back head, back head gusset

Painted-Face Jester

(Size: 21 inches; Difficulty Level: 3)

MATERIALS

☐ 1/2 yard forest green mohair, 3/4" pile

☐ One 12" x 15" white mohair, 3/4" pile, for head and paws

☐ One 12" x 12" white 100% felt for paws

☐ One 10" x 15" piece of fabric for hat and collars

☐ One pair of 8 or 10mm glass or plastic eyes

☐ Five 1½" joint sets for head, arms, and legs

☐ #3 black pearl cotton for nose and mouth

☐ Sewing-machine thread for seams, color to match fabric

☐ Polyester fiberfill for stuffing, excelsior for head (optional)

☐ Nylon upholstery thread for attaching eyes and closing seams

☐ Acrylic paint for face

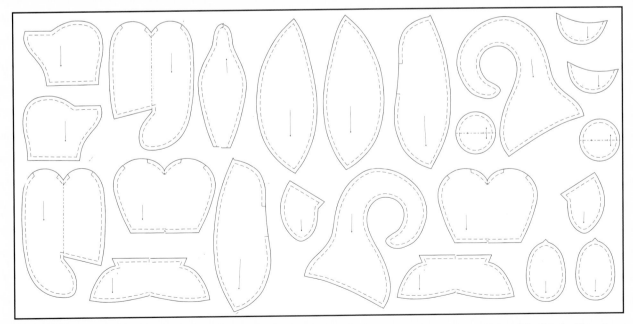

This diagram represents all of the pattern pieces required to complete this bear, laid out in the straight of the fabric. More than one piece of fabric may be required for laying out the pattern pieces.

INSTRUCTIONS

1

Sew side heads together from nose down to neck edge.

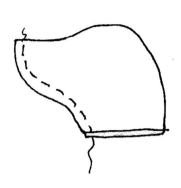

2

Sew center head gusset to side head section.

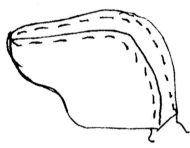

3

Sew a neck facing to the bottom of each side head.

When the head is stuffed and the neck joint is installed (cotter pin, fender washer, and fiber disk), close the facing around the cotter pin and sew closed.

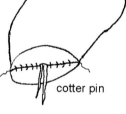

cotter pin

4

Fold ear in half and sew, cut the center section for turning.

cut and leave open

5

Sew paws to arms on both right and left arms.

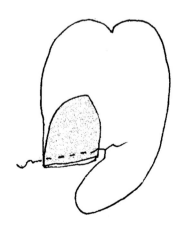

6

Fold arm and sew, leaving the top open for stuffing.

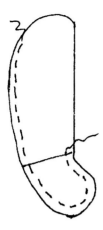

7

Sew foot to leg, for both right and left legs.

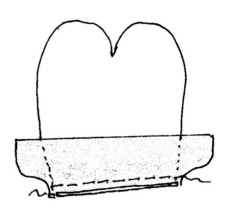

8

Fold leg in half and sew, leaving the top open for stuffing.

Baste sole to foot, then machine-sew around basting.

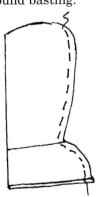 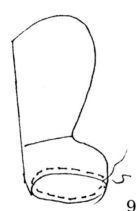

9

Sew two body fronts together at center front seam. Sew two body backs together at center back seam, leaving the center open for stuffing.

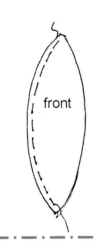

front

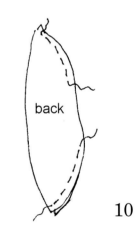

back

10

Sew body front section and body back section together at side seams. The head will attach at the tab on the neck edge. Refer to the Basic Directions to complete the head and attach the head, arms, and legs to the body. Stuff and close the open seams.

insert head here

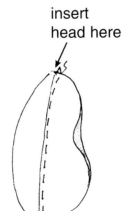

11

Sew two hat pieces together. Before attaching the hat to top of head, insert padded wire or pipe cleaners so the hat will stand up. Sew one end of the wire to the top of the head and the other end to the top of the hat.

pipe cleaner

12

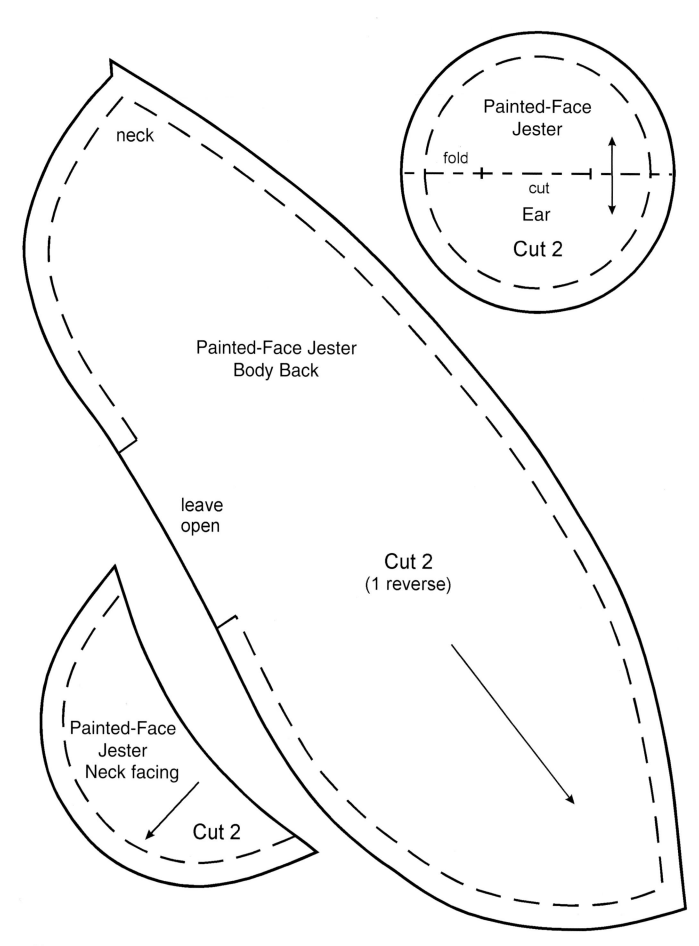

neck

Painted-Face Jester
Body Back

leave
open

Cut 2
(1 reverse)

Painted-Face
Jester
Neck facing

Cut 2

Painted-Face
Jester

fold

cut

Ear

Cut 2

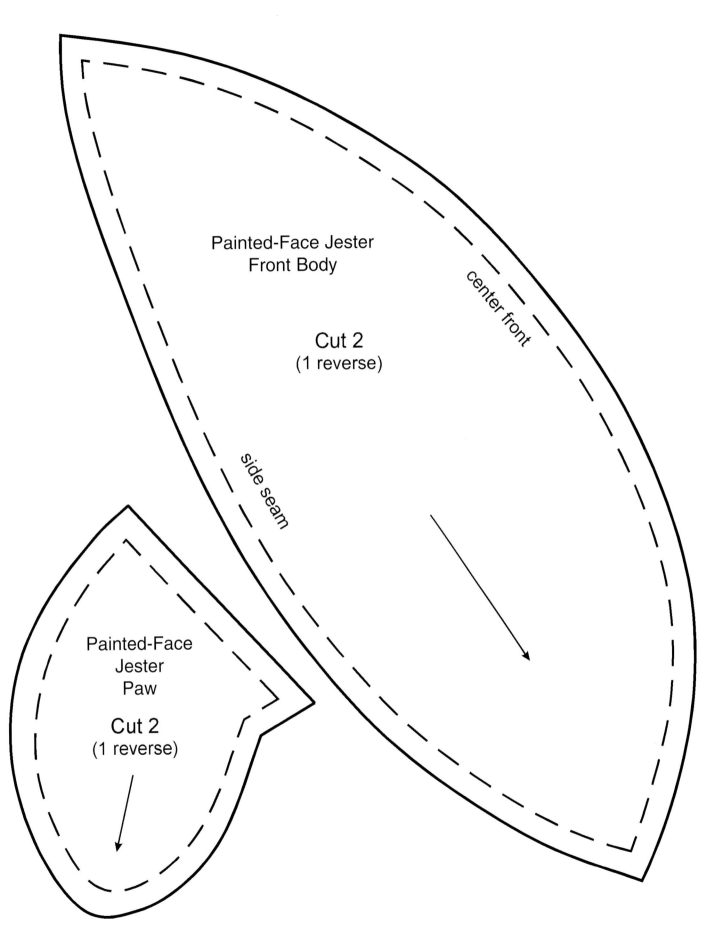

Painted-Face Jester
Front Body

Cut 2
(1 reverse)

center front

side seam

Painted-Face
Jester
Paw

Cut 2
(1 reverse)

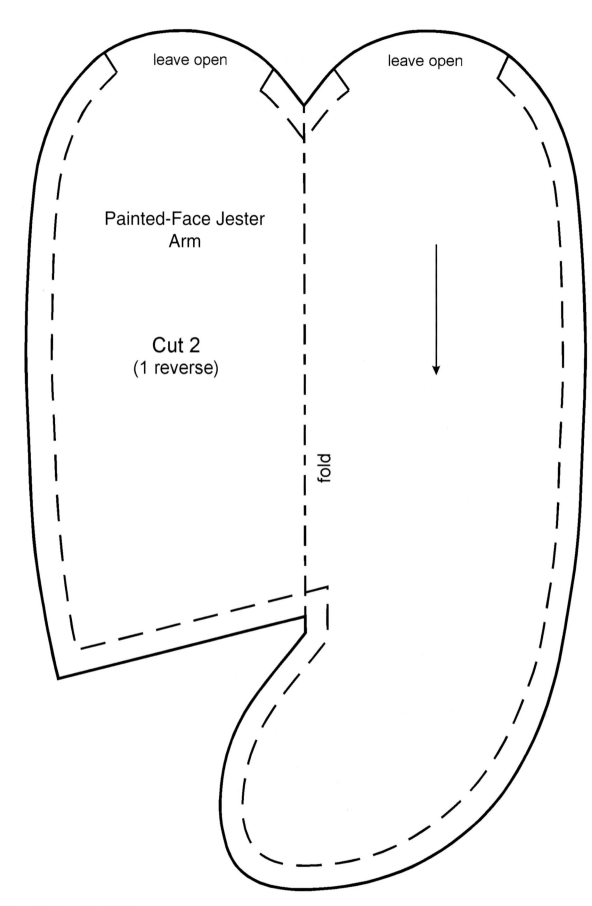

leave open

leave open

Painted-Face Jester
Arm

Cut 2
(1 reverse)

fold

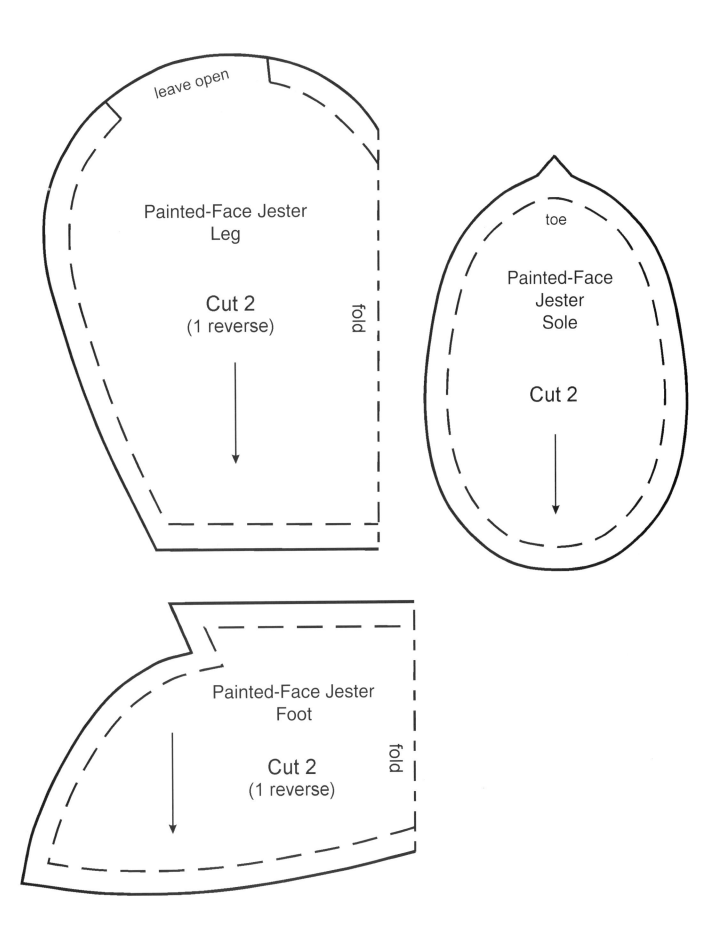

leave open

Painted-Face Jester
Leg

Cut 2
(1 reverse)

fold

toe

Painted-Face
Jester
Sole

Cut 2

Painted-Face Jester
Foot

Cut 2
(1 reverse)

fold

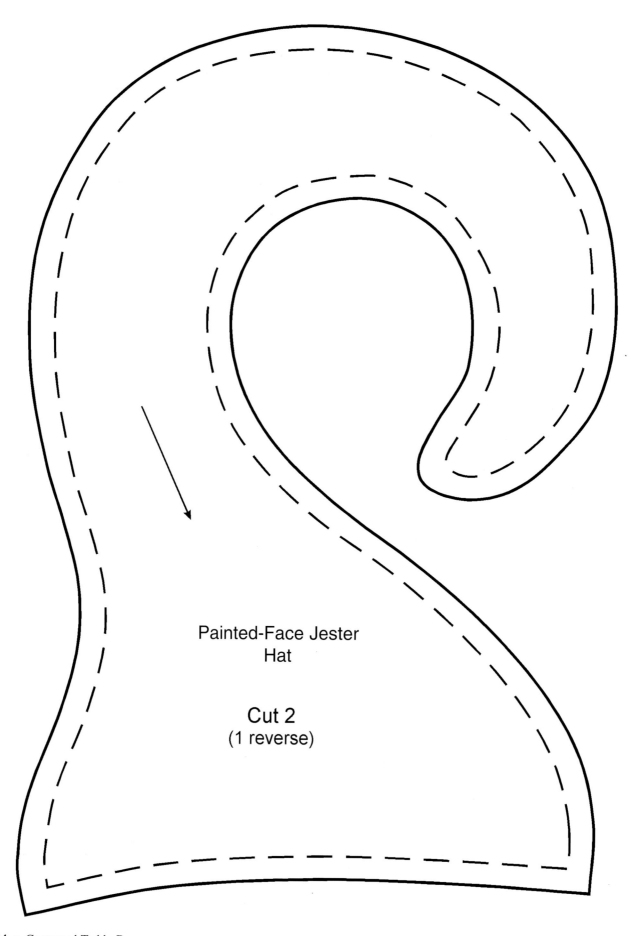

Painted-Face Jester
Hat

Cut 2
(1 reverse)

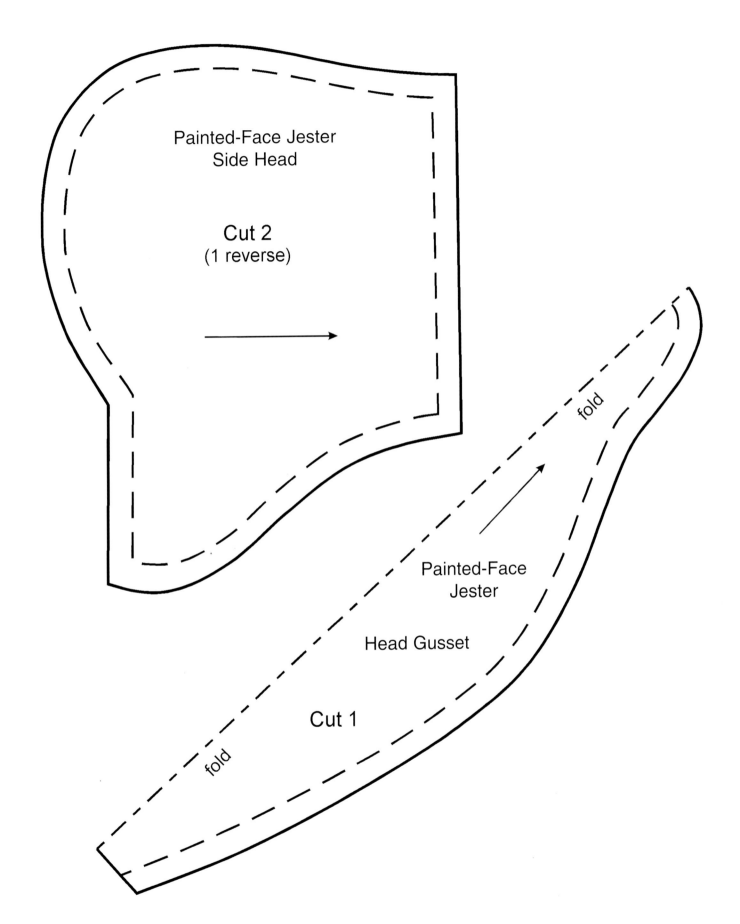

Painted-Face Jester
Side Head

Cut 2
(1 reverse)

fold

Painted-Face
Jester

Head Gusset

Cut 1

fold

Ming Panda

(Size: 20 inches; Difficulty Level: 4)

MATERIALS

- ☐ 1/4 yard black mohair, 3/4" pile
- ☐ 1/4 yard gold mohair, 3/4" pile
- ☐ One 7" x 7" piece of black 100% wool felt for paws and soles
- ☐ One 13" x 13" piece of gold 100% wool felt for hat band
- ☐ One 3" x 6" piece of 100% wool felt in each color, red and dark-green, for hat crown
- ☐ One pair 8mm black glass eyes
- ☐ Two fancy gold beads to decorate top of hat crown
- ☐ Five 2½" T-cotter pin joint sets for arms and legs
- ☐ One 3¼" T-cotter pin joint set for double-jointed head
- ☐ #3 black pearl cotton for nose
- ☐ Sewing-machine thread for seams, color to match fabric
- ☐ Waxed thread for attaching eyes
- ☐ Nylon upholstery thread for closing seams
- ☐ Polyester fiberfill stuffing

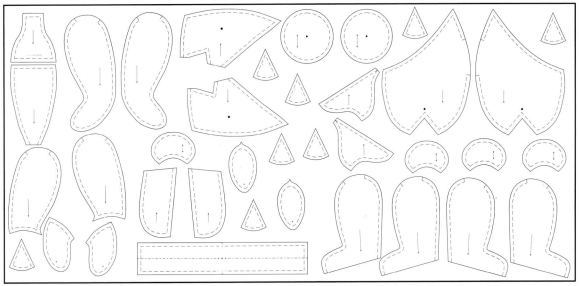

This diagram represents all of the pattern pieces required to complete this bear, laid out in the straight of the fabric. More than one piece of fabric may be required for laying out the pattern pieces.

INSTRUCTIONS

1

2

Sew the two face pieces to the face gusset. Fold the face pieces together and sew from the nose down to the neck.

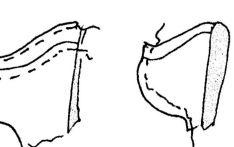

3

Sew the two side heads to the side head gusset.

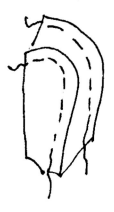

4

Sew a fabric disk to the face section and the side head section. Leave the bottom of the side-head section open for stuffing and attaching.

5

Joint the front-face section (shown here) to the back-head section (shown in step 7) to complete the head.

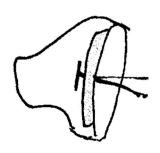

6

This is the back-head section described in step 6.

To complete the head, stuff the two head sections and install the head joint.

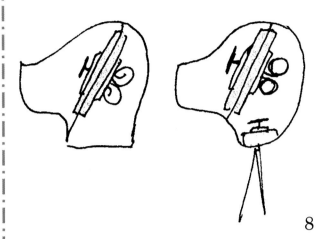

7

8

Sew the top and bottom sections of the body together. Sew a left and a right body.

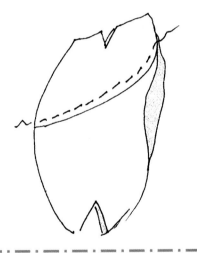

Sew the front seams together. Sew the back seams, leaving the center back open for jointing and stuffing.

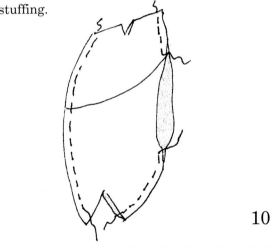

9

10

Sew darts at the neck edge and the bottom of the body.

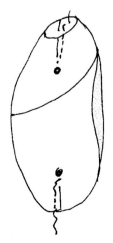

Sew paw to inner arm, sew outer arm and inner arm together for both arms. Leave the tops open for jointing and stuffing.

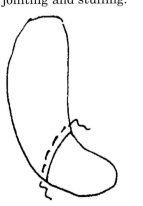

11

12

Position two leg pieces, pile sides together, and sew, leaving the top open for jointing and stuffing. Baste the sole to the bottom of the leg, then machine-sew the sole to the leg.

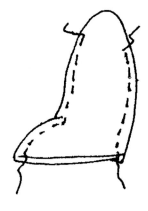 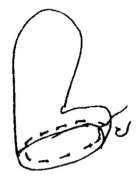

13

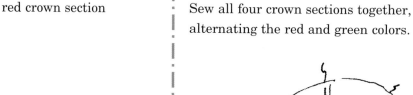

Sew one green and one red crown section together, 4 times.

Sew all four crown sections together, alternating the red and green colors.

14

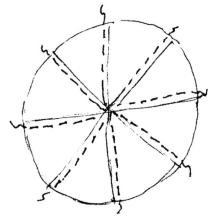

15

Fold the hat band piece and sew on to the crown section. Zig-zag the seam and turn inside out.

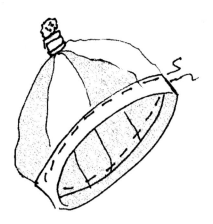 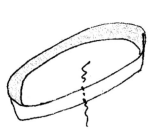

16

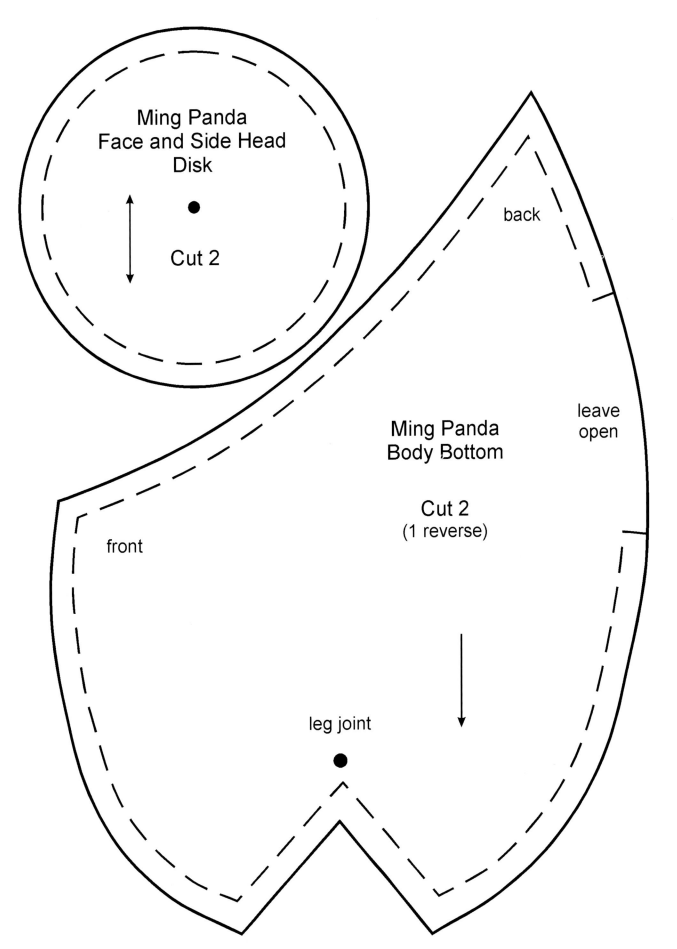

Ming Panda
Face and Side Head
Disk

Cut 2

Ming Panda
Body Bottom

Cut 2
(1 reverse)

back

leave
open

front

leg joint

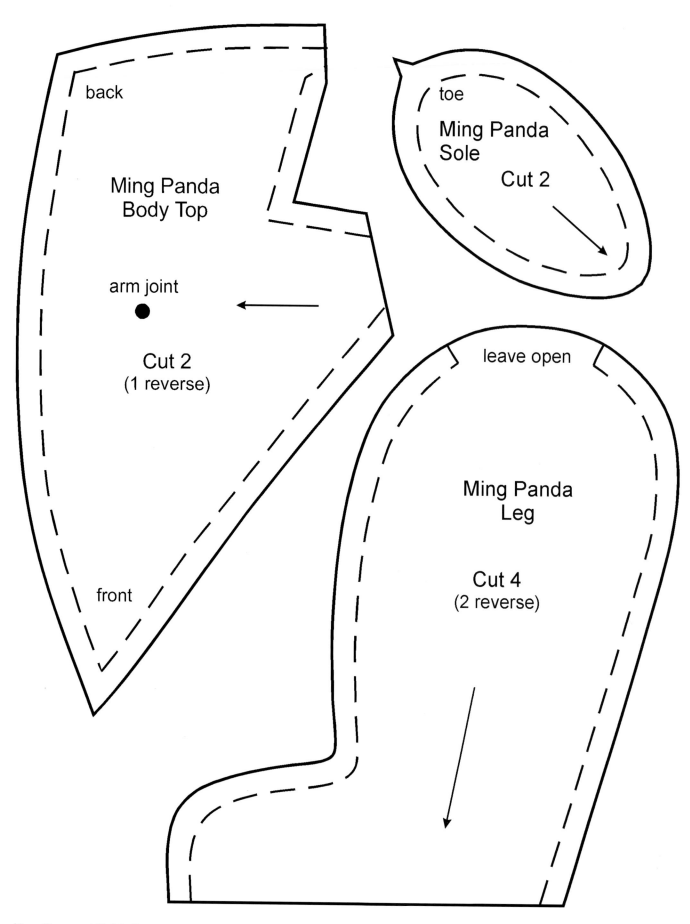

back

Ming Panda
Body Top

arm joint

Cut 2
(1 reverse)

front

toe

Ming Panda
Sole

Cut 2

leave open

Ming Panda
Leg

Cut 4
(2 reverse)

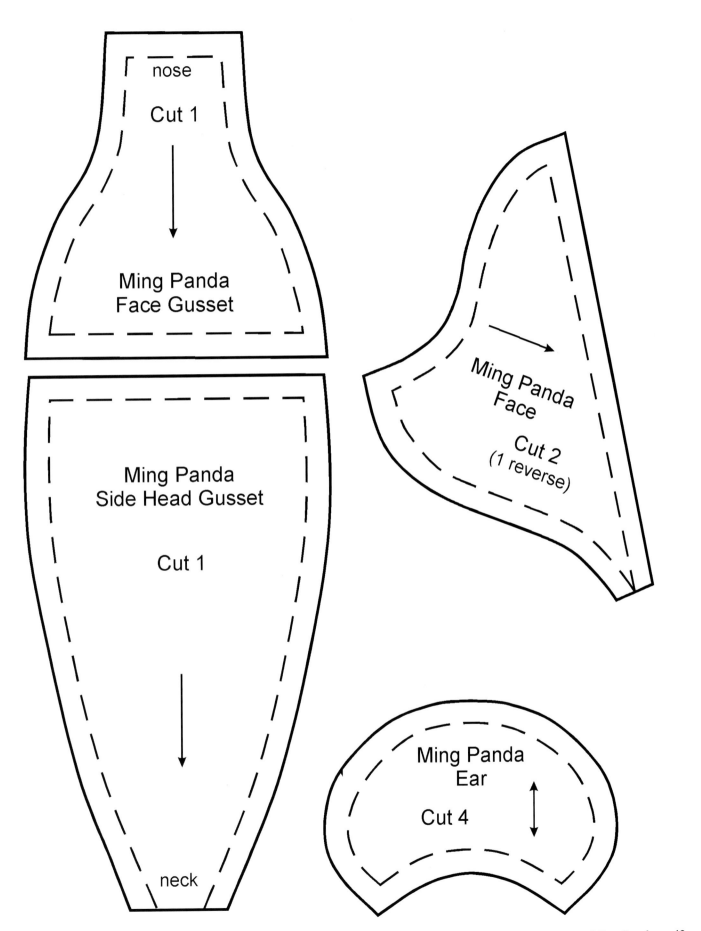

nose

Cut 1

Ming Panda
Face Gusset

Ming Panda
Side Head Gusset

Cut 1

neck

Ming Panda
Face

Cut 2
(1 reverse)

Ming Panda
Ear

Cut 4

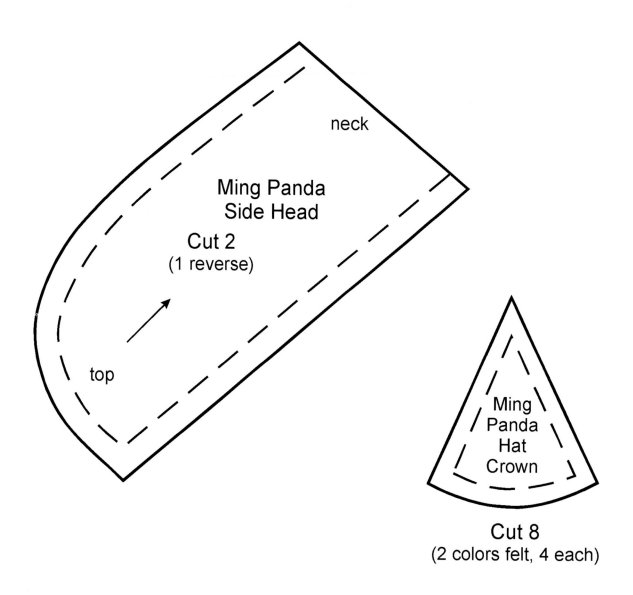

neck

Ming Panda
Side Head

Cut 2
(1 reverse)

top

Ming
Panda
Hat
Crown

Cut 8
(2 colors felt, 4 each)

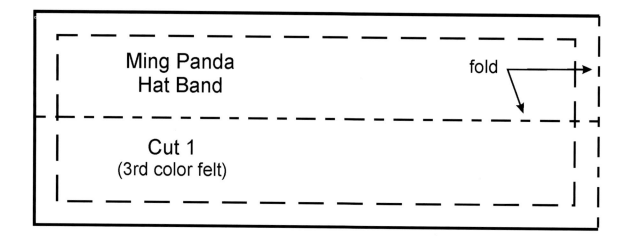

Ming Panda
Hat Band

fold

Cut 1
(3rd color felt)

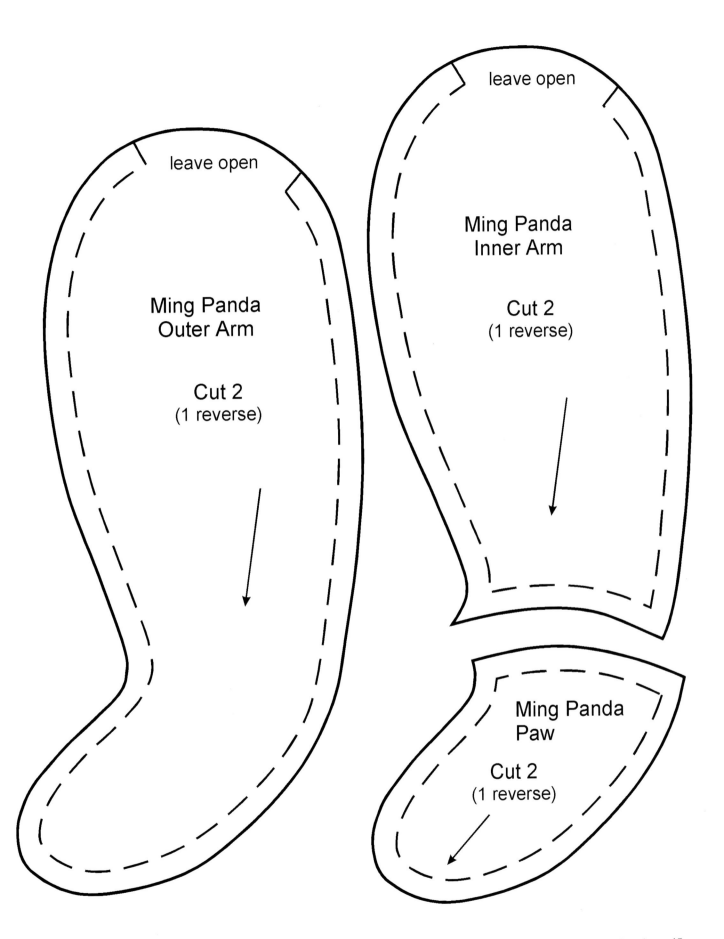

leave open

Ming Panda
Outer Arm

Cut 2
(1 reverse)

leave open

Ming Panda
Inner Arm

Cut 2
(1 reverse)

Ming Panda
Paw

Cut 2
(1 reverse)

Santa

(Size: 12 inches; Difficulty Level: 5)

MATERIALS

- ☐ 1/4 yard red mohair or coat wool, 1/4" pile, hat
- ☐ One 30" x 1" of white mohair, 1/4" pile, for jacket trim, hat
- ☐ Two pieces 12" x 12" black upholstery fabric for boots
- ☐ One piece 9" x 9" beige 100% wool felt for paws
- ☐ Small piece beige mohair, 1/2" pile, for head, paws
- ☐ 5 small gold beads for buttons
- ☐ 1 large bead for hat
- ☐ One small belt buckle
- ☐ One pair 7mm glass or plastic eyes
- ☐ Five 1" T-cotter pin joints for head, arms, and legs
- ☐ #5 black pearl cotton for nose and mouth
- ☐ Sewing-machine thread for seams, color to match fabric
- ☐ Polyester fiberfill for stuffing
- ☐ Nylon upholstery thread for attaching eyes and closing seams

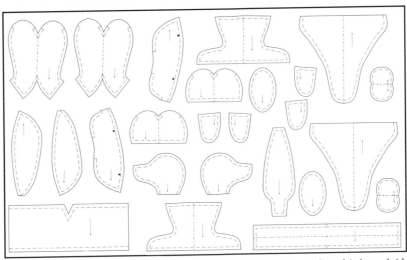

This diagram represents all of the pattern pieces required to complete this bear, laid out in the straight of the fabric. More than one piece of fabric may be required for laying out the pattern pieces.

INSTRUCTIONS

Sew two side heads to center gusset.

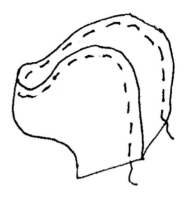

Fold center head gusset and sew from nose down to neck edge.

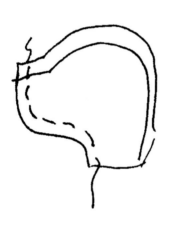

Fold ear and sew. Cut center section for turning.

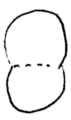

cut and leave open

Sew one mohair and one felt paw to each arm for both right and left arms. Make sure the felt paw is on the inside of the arm.

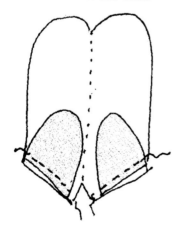

Fold arm in half and sew, leaving the top open for stuffing.

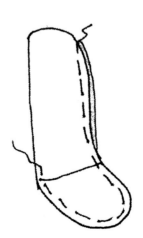

Sew top of leg piece to the boot piece for both legs.

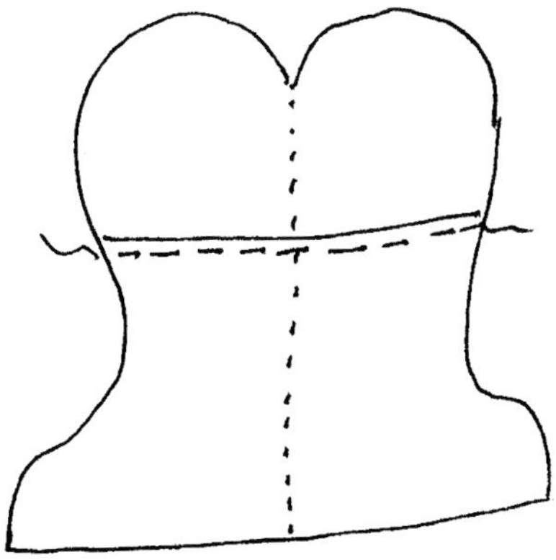

7

Fold leg in half and sew, leaving the top open for stuffing.

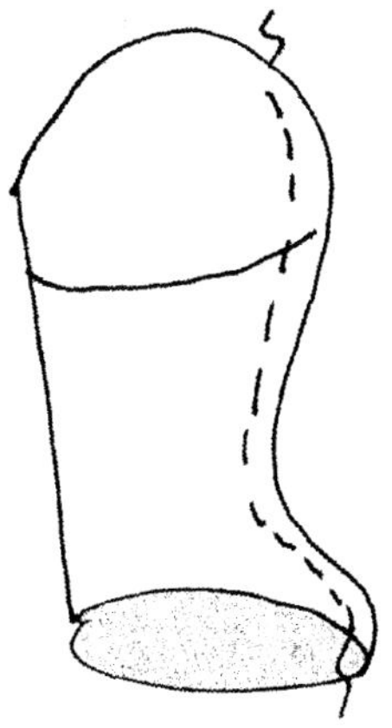

8

For both boots, baste sole to bottom of boot, then machine-sew.

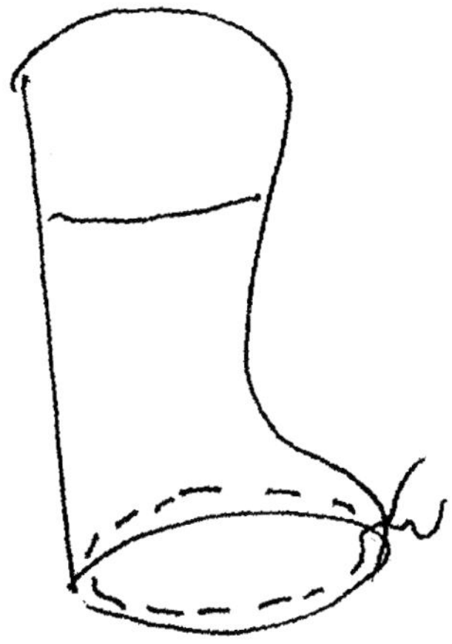

9

Sew two body front pieces together.

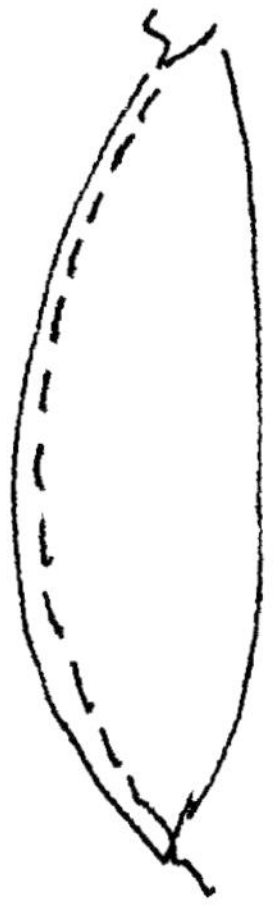

10

Sew two body back pieces together.

11

Sew body front section and body back section together at side seam.

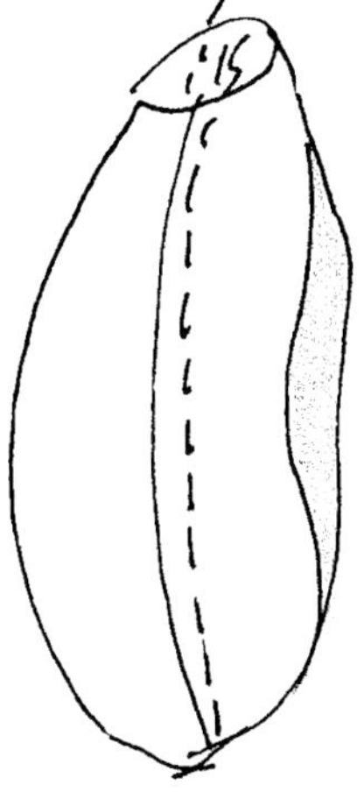

12

Fold hat together and sew at side seam.

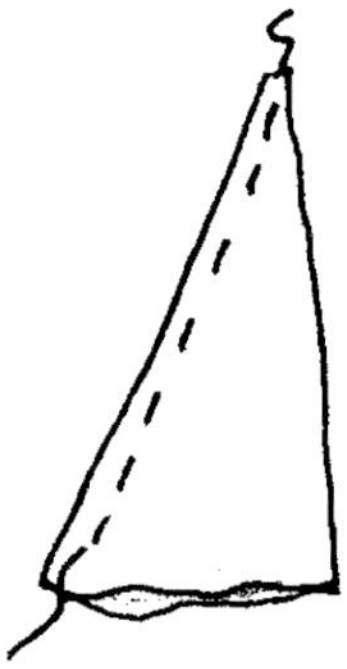

Turn hat right side out, sew trim on bottom of hat and sew bell on top of hat.

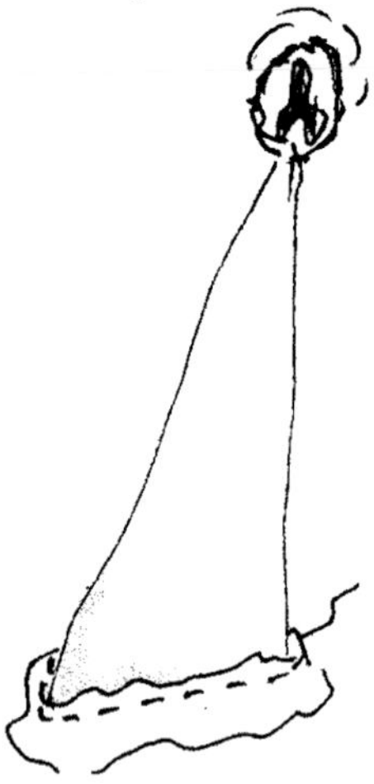

13

14

Sew dart in jacket skirt.

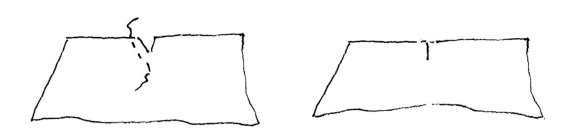

15

Top-stitch jacket band.

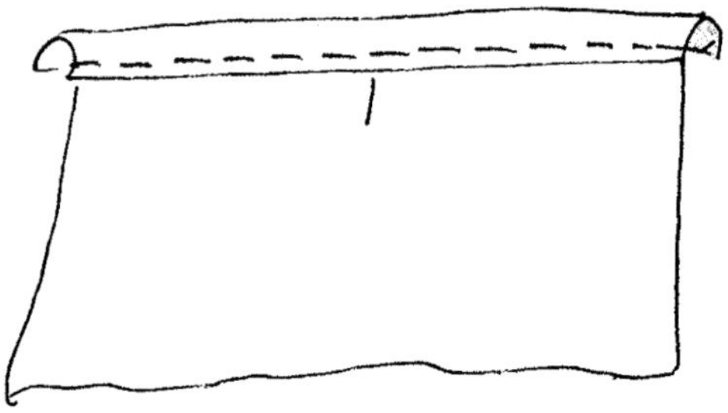

Sew band to the top of the jacket skirt.

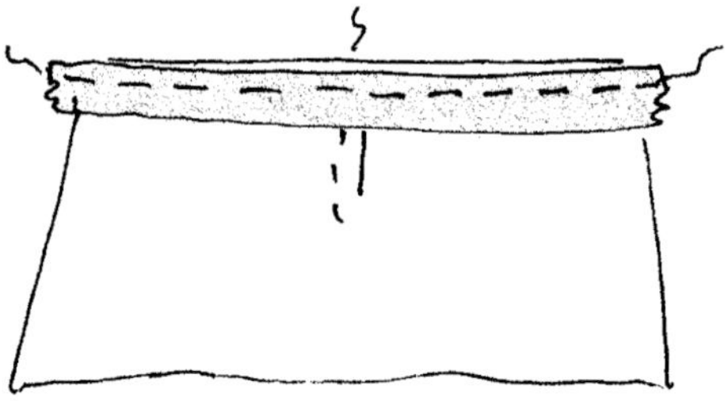

16

17

Attach belt buckle to jacket band (look at a real belt to see how it's done). Attach skirt to finished bear at waist over front center seam.

Drape the jacket skirt around the bear and sew the side of jacket skirt with buckle over the previous attachment.

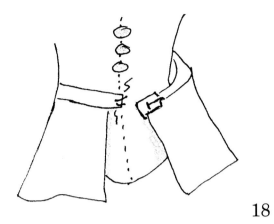

18

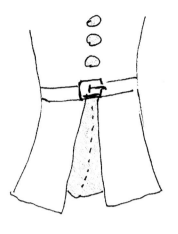

19

Attach beard and mustache after sewing face on bear.

board

mustache

20

21

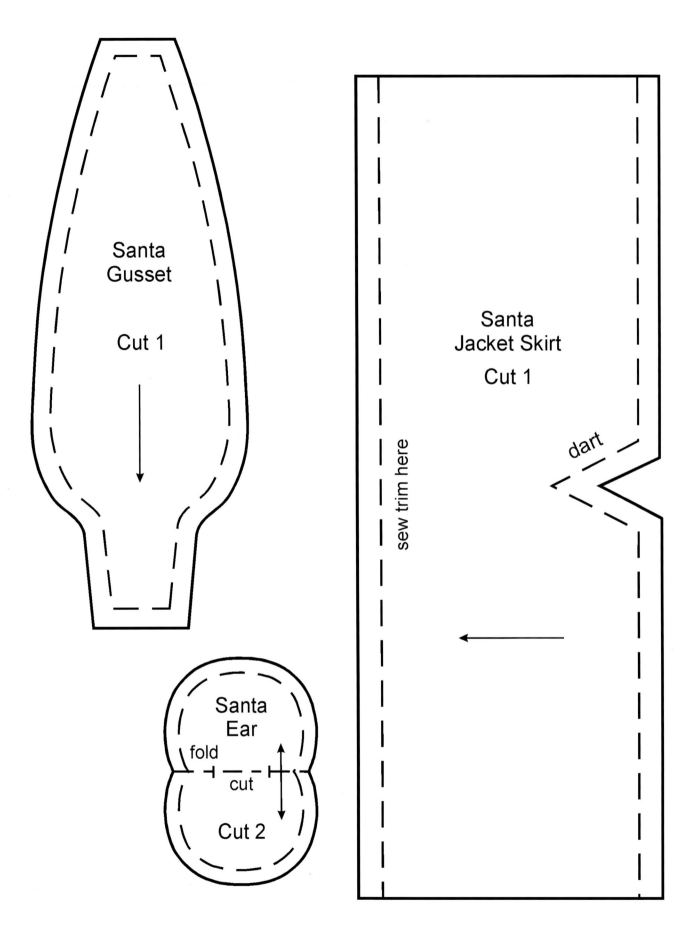

Santa
Gusset

Cut 1

Santa
Jacket Skirt
Cut 1

sew trim here

dart

Santa
Ear

fold

cut

Cut 2

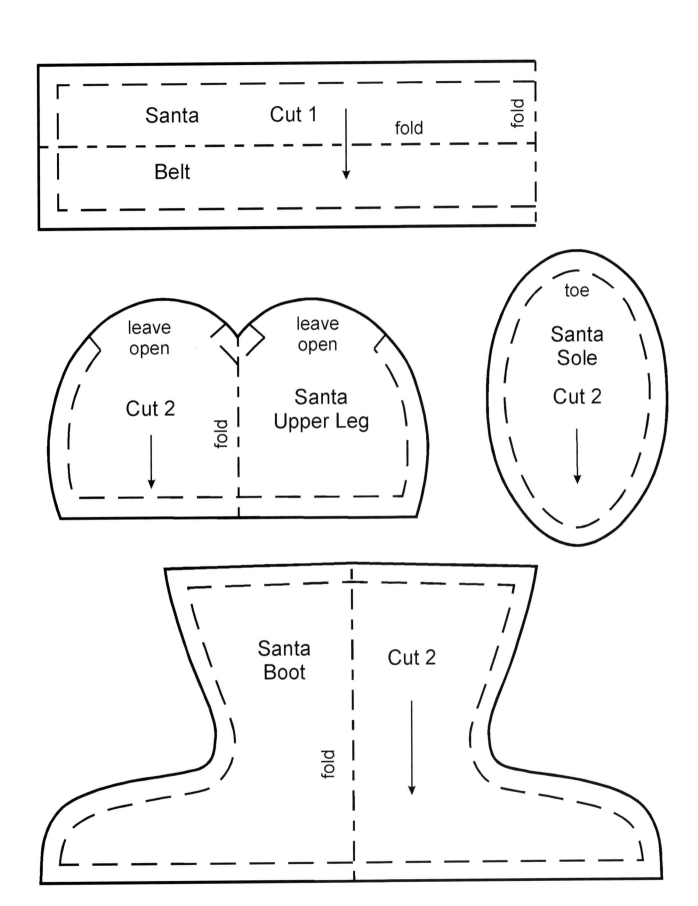

Santa   Cut 1

fold

fold

Belt

leave open

leave open

Cut 2

Santa Upper Leg

fold

toe

Santa Sole

Cut 2

Santa Boot   Cut 2

fold

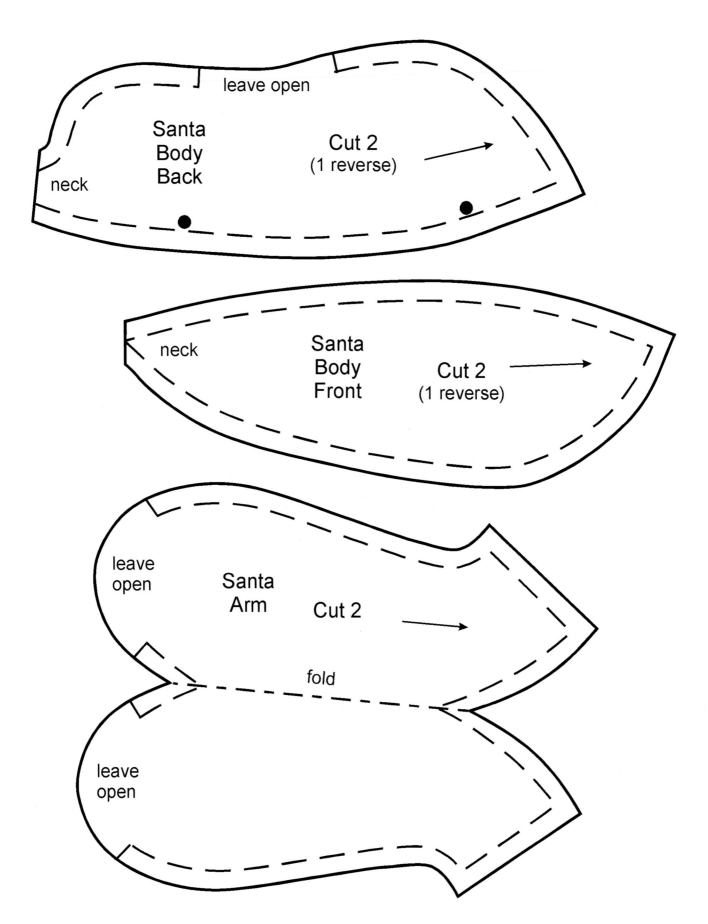

leave open

Santa
Body
Back

Cut 2
(1 reverse)

neck

neck

Santa
Body
Front

Cut 2
(1 reverse)

leave
open

Santa
Arm

Cut 2

fold

leave
open

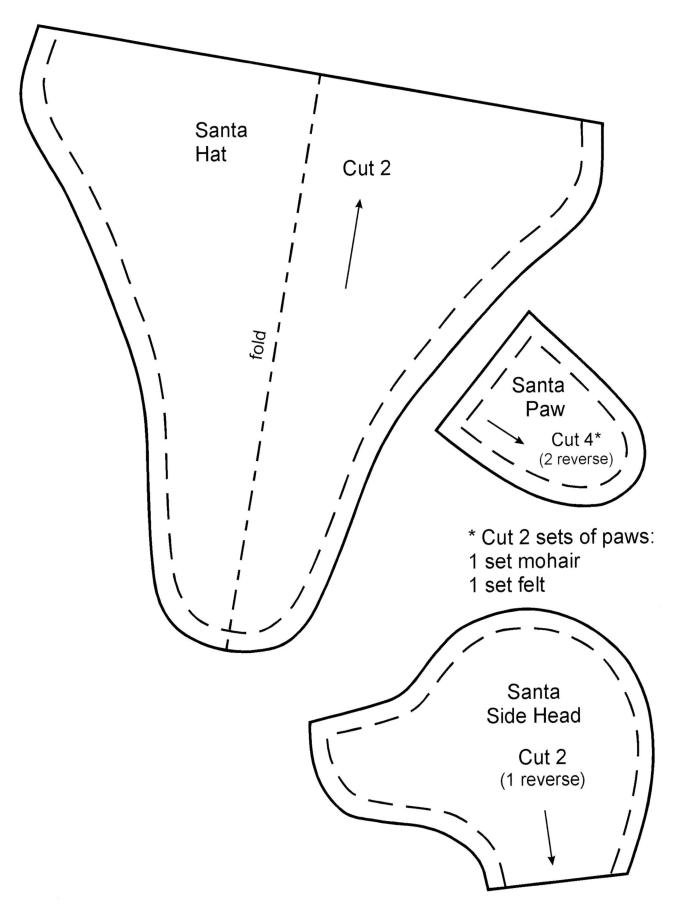

Santa
Hat

Cut 2

fold

Santa
Paw

Cut 4*
(2 reverse)

* Cut 2 sets of paws:
1 set mohair
1 set felt

Santa
Side Head

Cut 2
(1 reverse)

Santa's Helper

(Size: 8 inches; Difficulty Level: 5)

MATERIALS

☐ One piece 12" x 8" green mohair, 1/8" pile, for body

☐ One piece 6" x 4" beige mohair, 1/4" pile, for head

☐ One piece 2" x 3½" beige 100% wool felt for paws

☐ One piece 5" x 5" red coat wool for shoes

☐ One piece 3" x 6" red 100% wool felt for hat

☐ Two pieces 1½" x 6" 100% wool felt for collar, one red, one green

☐ Four small gold beads for decorating hat and front of body.

☐ Two small glass or plastic beads for eyes

☐ One bag of plastic balloon ties for joints (available at craft stores)

☐ Five medium T-cotter pins

☐ Ten small fender washers

☐ #5 black pearl cotton for nose

☐ Sewing-machine thread for seams, color to match fabric

☐ Nylon thread for attaching eyes and closing seams

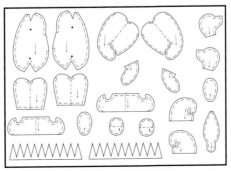

This diagram represents all of the pattern pieces required to complete this bear, laid out in the straight of the fabric. More than one piece of fabric may be required for laying out the pattern pieces.

INSTRUCTIONS

1

Sew two side heads together, starting at nose down to the neck edge.

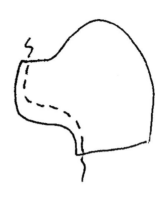

2

Sew head gusset to head sides.

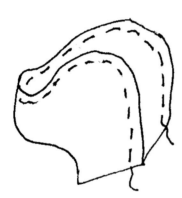

3

Fold ears and sew closed. Cut a small opening in the center of fold for turning the ears inside out.

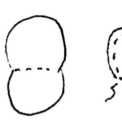

cut and leave open

4

Sew paws to inner arms, both right and left sides.

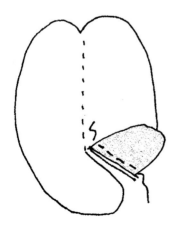

5

Fold arms in half and sew, leaving the top open for stuffing.

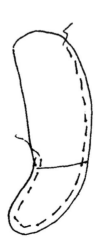

6

Sew foot to bottom edge of leg. Fold leg in half and sew, leaving the top open for stuffing.

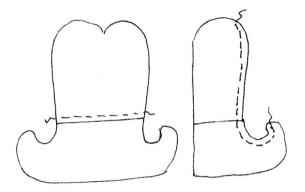

7

Sew the sole to the bottom of foot. Baste the sole to the bottom of the leg then machine-sew the sole to the leg.

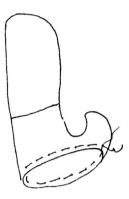

8

Sew two body pieces together, front seam and back seam, leaving the center back open for stuffing. Sew the darts on both left and right sides of body.

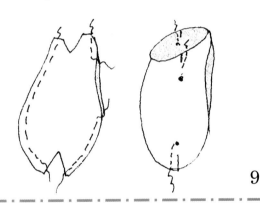

9

Stuff the head and insert the T-cotter pin, fender washer and disk. The disks for this small bear are balloon ties, which are small plastic disks with a hole in the center. Gather the neck edge over the disk and close the seam.

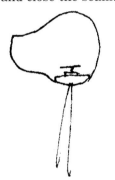

10

Gather the neck edge of the body to a small opening. Insert the T-cotter pin of the head through the body neck opening, then through a disk and fender washer. Join body and head together.

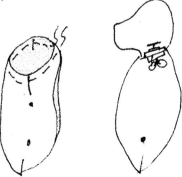

11

Join the arms and legs to the body. Stuff and close. Sew on buttons. Cut two felt collars. Place one collar around the neck and tack in back. Attach the second collar the same way and adjust the position so the collar points alternate red and green.

Sew two pieces of hat together. Turn right side out and attach to head.

12

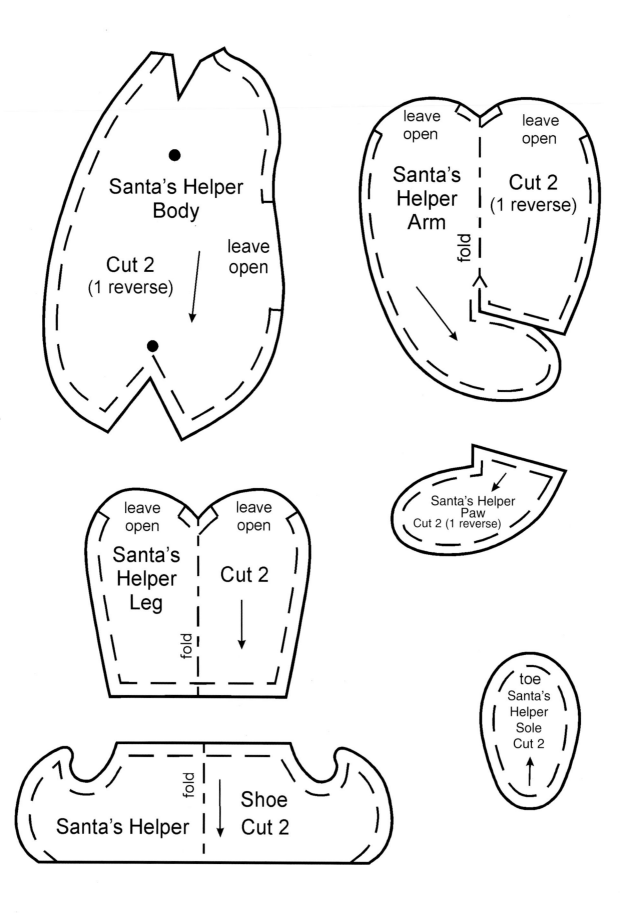

Santa's Helper
Body

Cut 2
(1 reverse)

leave
open

leave
open

leave
open

Santa's
Helper
Arm

Cut 2
(1 reverse)

fold

Santa's Helper
Paw
Cut 2 (1 reverse)

leave
open

leave
open

Santa's
Helper
Leg

Cut 2

fold

toe
Santa's
Helper
Sole
Cut 2

fold

Santa's Helper

Shoe
Cut 2

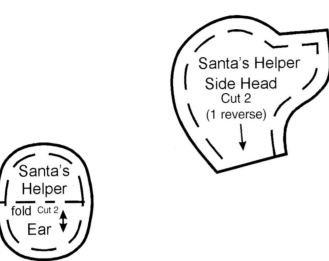

Santa's Helper
Side Head
Cut 2
(1 reverse)

Santa's
Helper
fold Cut 2
Ear

Santa's
Helper
Head
Gusset
Cut 1

Cut 2
(1 reverse)

Santa's
Helper
Hat

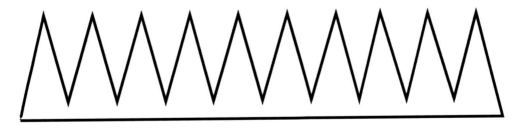

Santa's Helper Collar (felt)
Cut 2 (one red, one green)

Santa with Bag

(Size: 20 inches; Difficulty Level: 6)

MATERIALS

☐ One piece 10" x 18" gold mohair, 1/2" pile, for head and paws

☐ 1/2 yard red mohair or wool, 1/4" pile

☐ One 3" x 50" of white lambs wool for trimming of jacket

☐ One piece 12" x 12" white upholstery fabric for boots

☐ 5 small gold bells for buttons

☐ 1 large bell for hat

☐ Small belt buckle

☐ One 9" x 9" gold 100% wool felt for paws

☐ One pair of 7mm glass or plastic eyes

☐ Five 2" T-cotter pin joint sets for head, arms, and legs

☐ #3 black pearl cotton for nose and mouth

☐ Sewing-machine thread for seams, color to match fabric

☐ Polyester fiberfill for stuffing

☐ Nylon upholstery thread for attaching eyes and closing seams

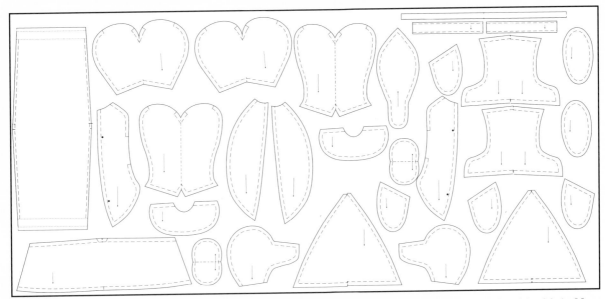

This diagram represents all of the pattern pieces required to complete this bear, laid out in the straight of the fabric. More than one piece of fabric may be required for laying out the pattern pieces.

INSTRUCTIONS

1

Sew side heads together starting at nose down to neck edge.

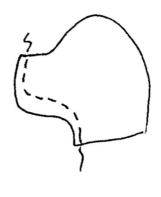

2

Sew side head section to head gusset.

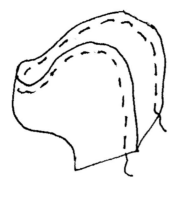

3

Fold ear, sew, and clip in center of fold for turning.

cut and leave open

4

Sew a mohair and an upholstery paw to arm for both right and left arms. Make sure the mohair paw is on the outside of the arm.

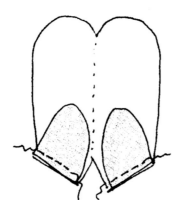

5

Fold arm in half and sew, leaving the top of arm open for stuffing.

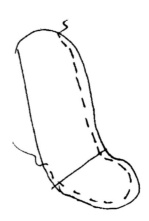

6

Sew top of leg to boot of leg for both right and left legs.

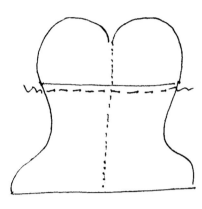

7

Fold leg in half and sew, leaving the top open for stuffing.

8

Baste sole to the bottom of boot, then machine-sew.

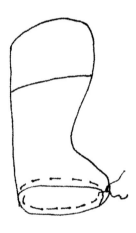

9

Sew two front sections of the body together at front seam.

10

Sew two back sections of the body in back, leaving the center open for stuffing.

11

Sew the body front and body back sections together at side seams.

12

Stuff head and attach to body. Attach arms and legs. Stuff and close. Sew on buttons.

Fold hat in half and sew on side seam. Sew trim on bottom of hat.

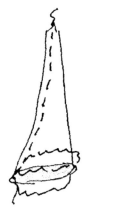

13

Sew trim on edges of both collar pieces. Attach collar around the neck.

14

Sew dart on jacket skirt.

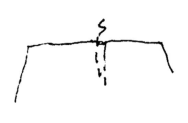

15

Sew band to top of jacket skirt.

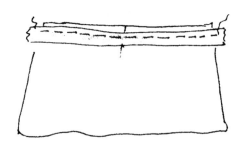

16

Top stitch band on right side.

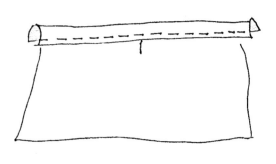

17

Attach belt buckle to jacket band (look at a real belt to see how it's done). Attach skirt to finished bear at waist over front center seam.

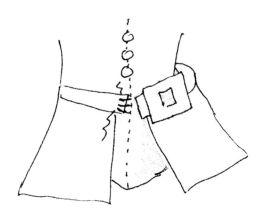

18

Drape the jacket skirt around the bear and sew the side of jacket skirt with buckle over the previous attachment.

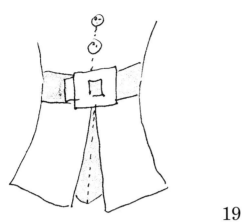

19

Sew casing to upper edge of bag on wrong side as indicated on the pattern.

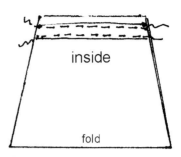

inside

fold

20

Fold bag in half and zig-zag side seams with right side out.

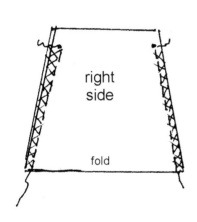

right side

fold

21

Thread straps through the casing and sew the straps together. Pull the straps so the joints are hidden inside the casing.

outside

22

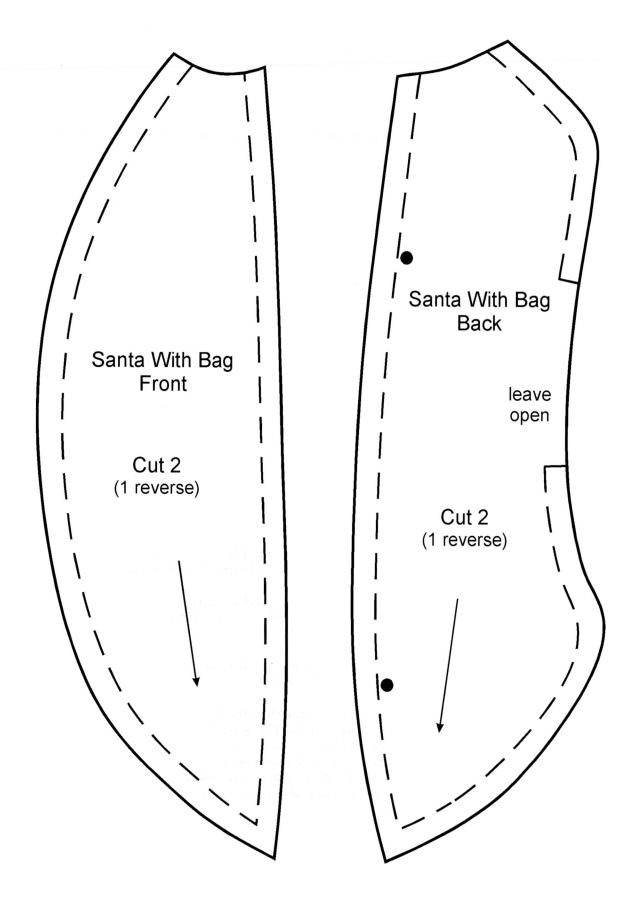

Santa With Bag
Front

Cut 2
(1 reverse)

Santa With Bag
Back

leave
open

Cut 2
(1 reverse)

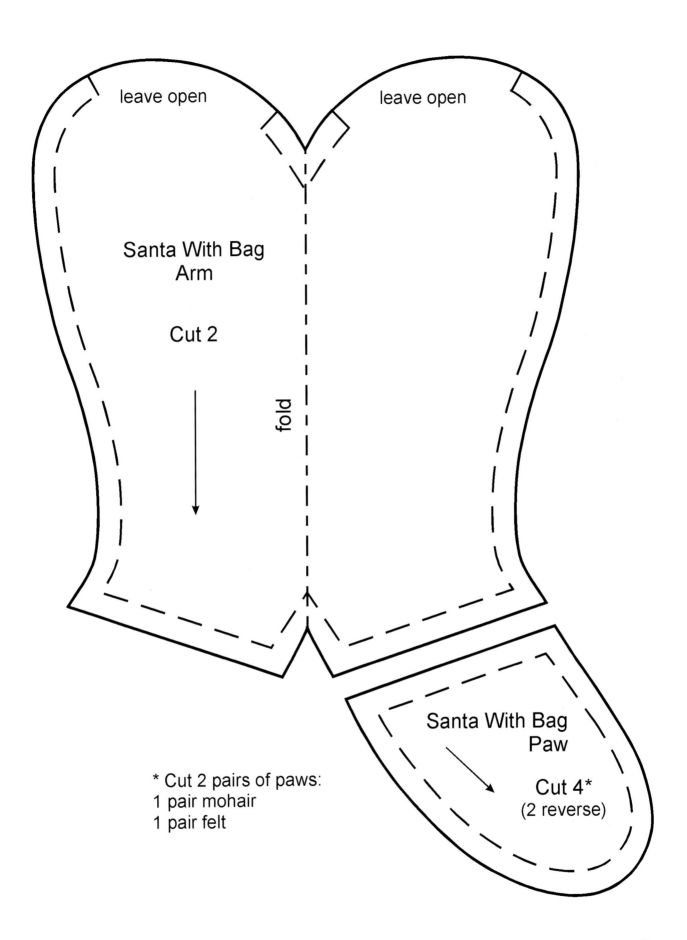

leave open

leave open

Santa With Bag
Arm

Cut 2

fold

* Cut 2 pairs of paws:
1 pair mohair
1 pair felt

Santa With Bag
Paw

Cut 4*
(2 reverse)

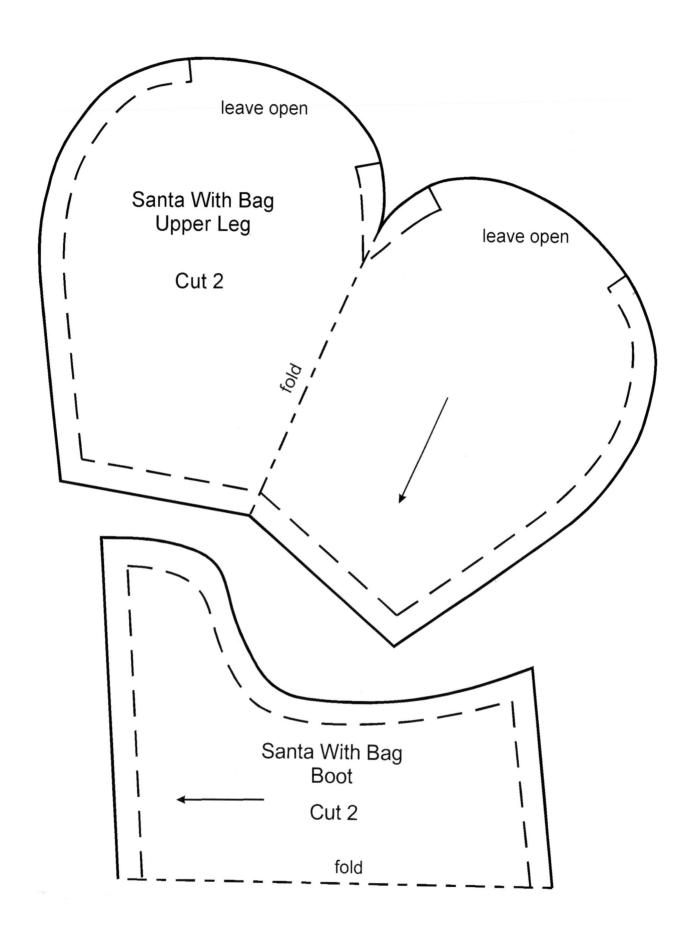

leave open

Santa With Bag
Upper Leg

Cut 2

leave open

fold

Santa With Bag
Boot

Cut 2

fold

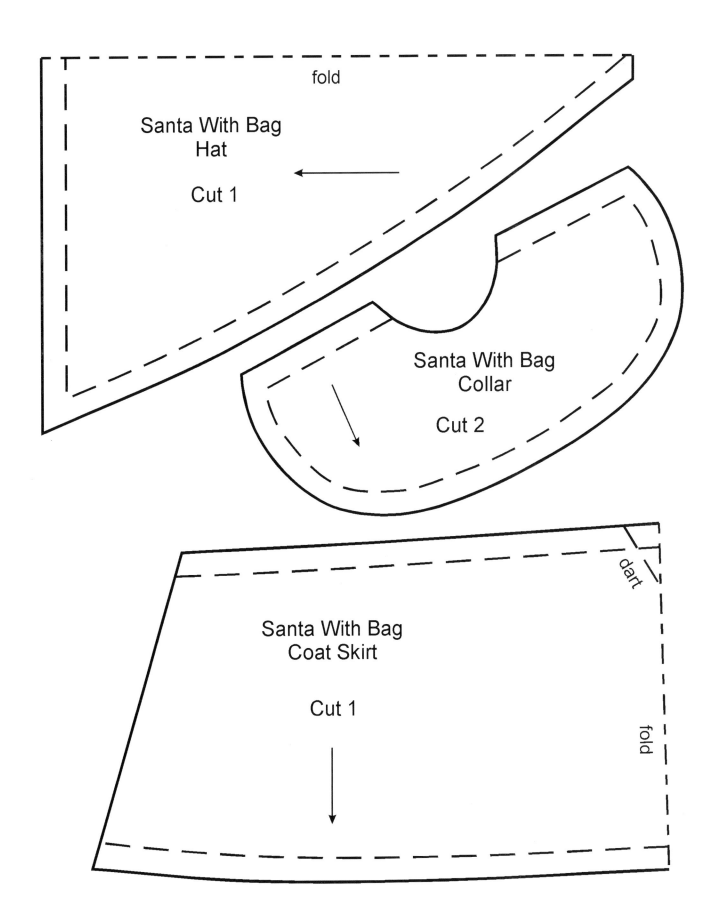

fold

Santa With Bag
Hat

Cut 1

Santa With Bag
Collar

Cut 2

Santa With Bag
Coat Skirt

Cut 1

dart

fold

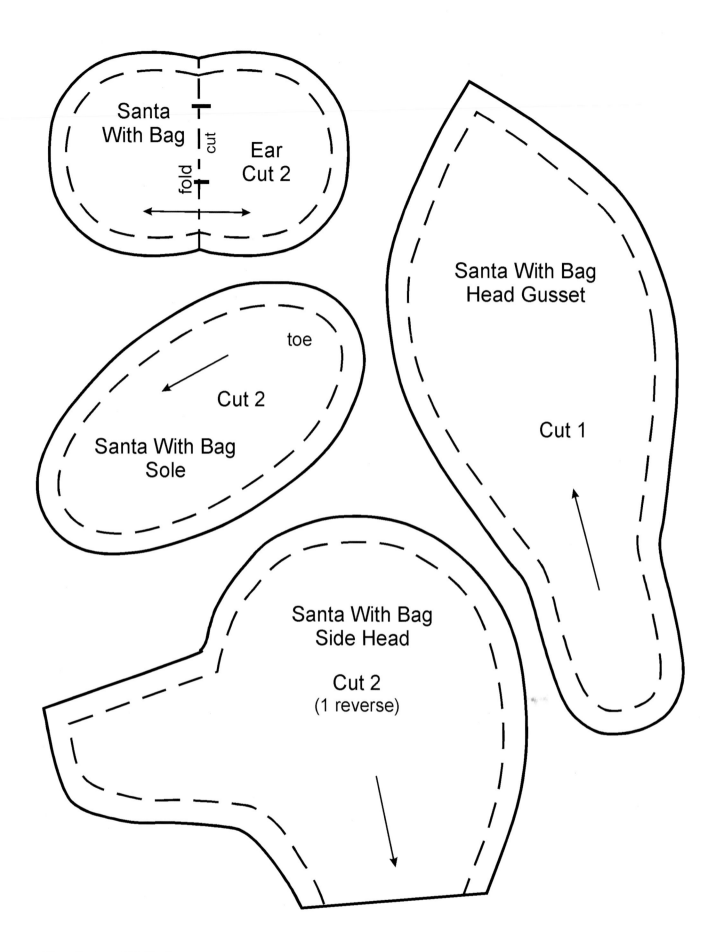

Santa
With Bag

fold

cut

Ear
Cut 2

toe

Cut 2

Santa With Bag
Sole

Santa With Bag
Head Gusset

Cut 1

Santa With Bag
Side Head

Cut 2
(1 reverse)

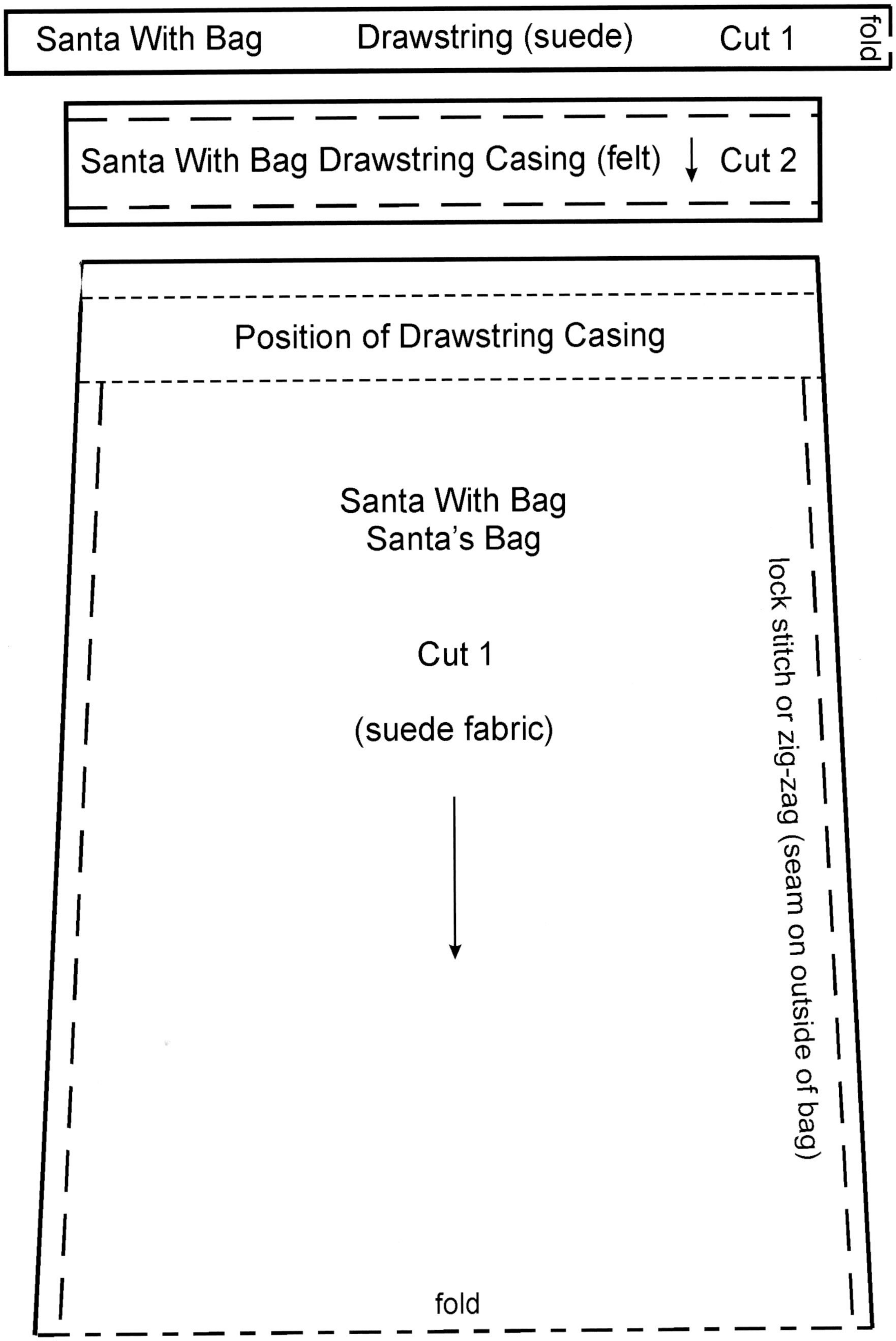

Santa With Bag   Drawstring (suede)   Cut 1   fold

Santa With Bag Drawstring Casing (felt) ↓ Cut 2

Position of Drawstring Casing

Santa With Bag
Santa's Bag

Cut 1

(suede fabric)

↓

lock stitch or zig-zag (seam on outside of bag)

fold

Clown-Face Jester

(Size: 14 inches; Difficulty Level: 7)

MATERIALS

☐ 1/4 yard each forest-green and mauve woven-back wool, 1/2" pile

☐ One scrap each white and gold mohair, 1/4" pile

☐ One 9" x 9" beige 100% wool felt for paws

☐ 3 large (1/2") gold buttons

☐ One pair of 6mm glass or plastic eyes

☐ Five 1½" T-cotter pin joint sets for head, legs, and arms

☐ #3 mauve and forest-green pearl cotton for face, nose and mouth

☐ Sewing-machine thread for seams, color to match fabric

☐ Polyester fiberfill for stuffing

☐ Nylon upholstery thread for attaching eyes and closing seams

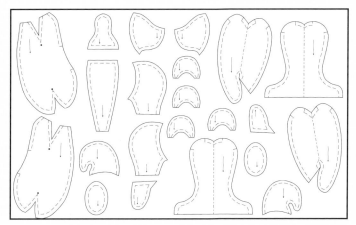

This diagram represents all of the pattern pieces required to complete this bear, laid out in the straight of the fabric. More than one piece of fabric may be required for laying out the pattern pieces.

INSTRUCTIONS

1

Sew two side head pieces to side head gusset.

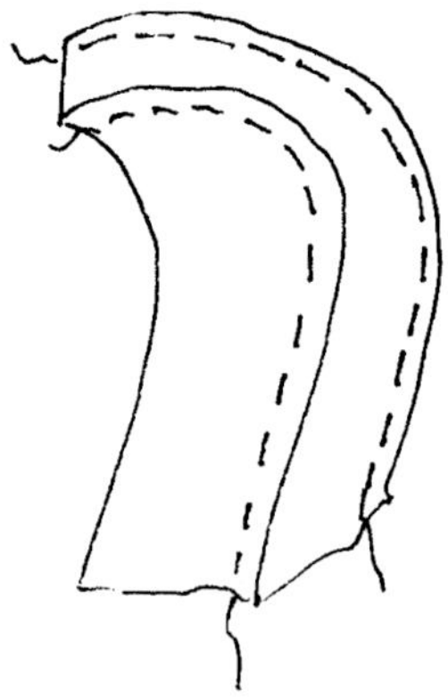

2

Sew two face pieces to face gusset piece.

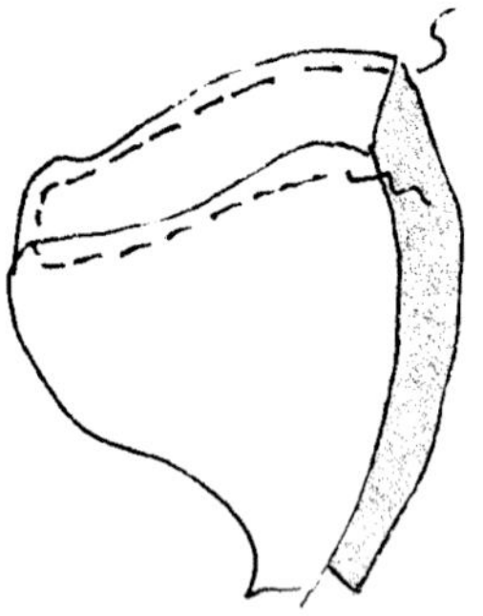

3

Sew face to side head.

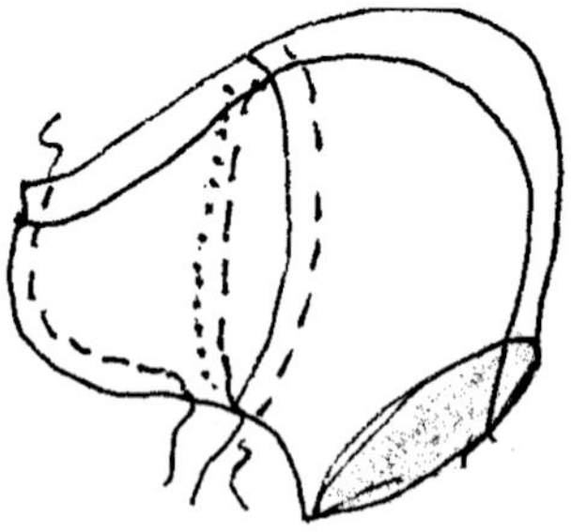

4

Sew two ears together, twice.

5

Sew a paw to the arm for both right and left arms.

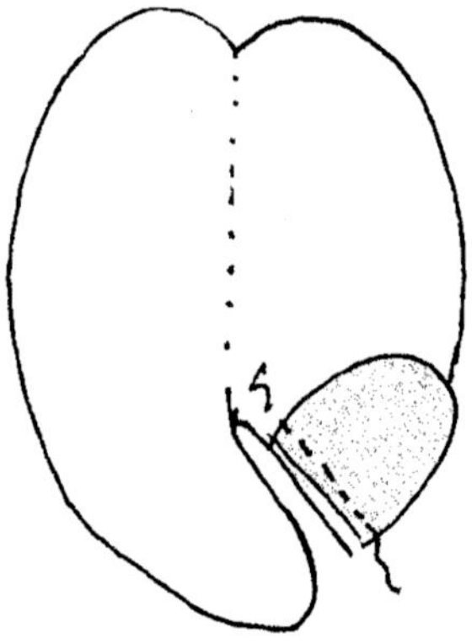

6

Fold arm in half and sew, leaving the top open for stuffing.

Fold legs in half and sew, leaving the top open for stuffing.

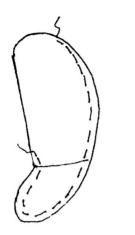

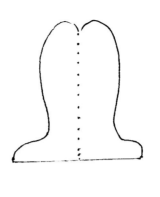
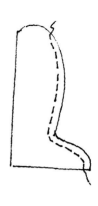

7

8

Baste sole into bottom of leg, then machine-sew.

Sew two body pieces together at front and back, leaving the center back open for stuffing. (One body piece is forest-green; the other is mauve.)

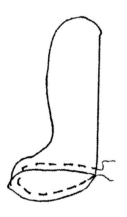

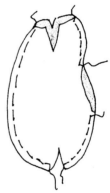

9

10

Sew darts at neck edge and bottom of body.

Stuff the head. Sew on nose and ears. Put hat pins in the eye locations. Refer to the illustrations in the Basic Directions. Sew two hat pieces together, one of each color.

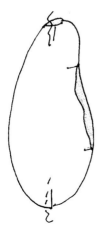

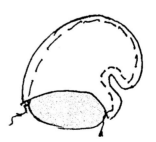

11

12

Stuff the hat lightly. Attach hat to head using a ladder stitch.

13

Embroider the face before attaching eyes.

14

Here is one stitching method for embroidery around the eyes.

15

Refer to the Basic Directions to attach the head, arms, and legs to the body. Stuff and close the open seams.

16

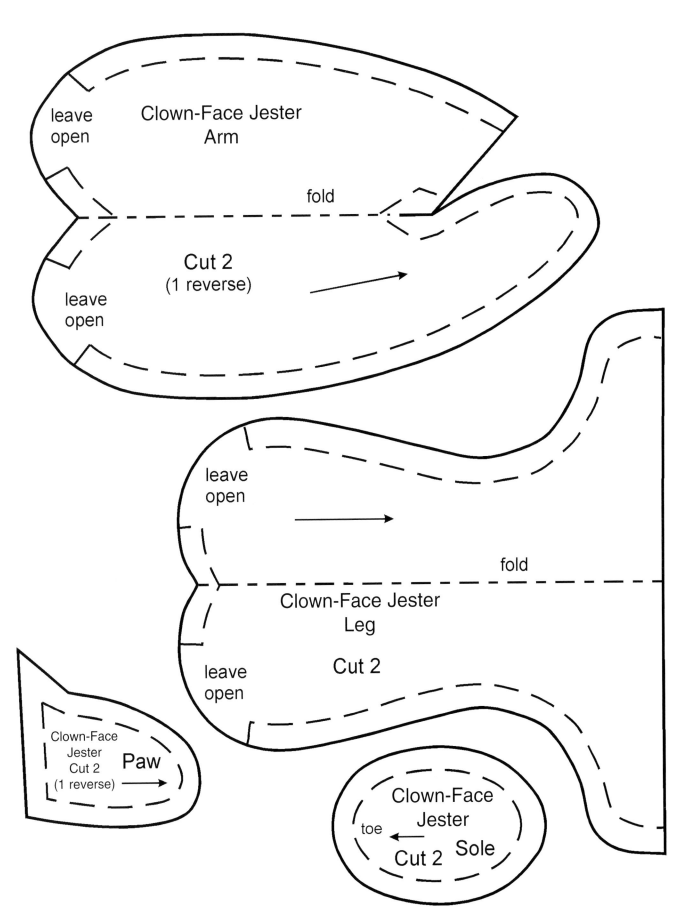

leave
open

Clown-Face Jester
Arm

fold

Cut 2
(1 reverse)

leave
open

leave
open

leave
open

Clown-Face Jester
Leg

fold

Cut 2

Clown-Face
Jester
Cut 2
(1 reverse)

Paw

Clown-Face
Jester

toe

Cut 2

Sole

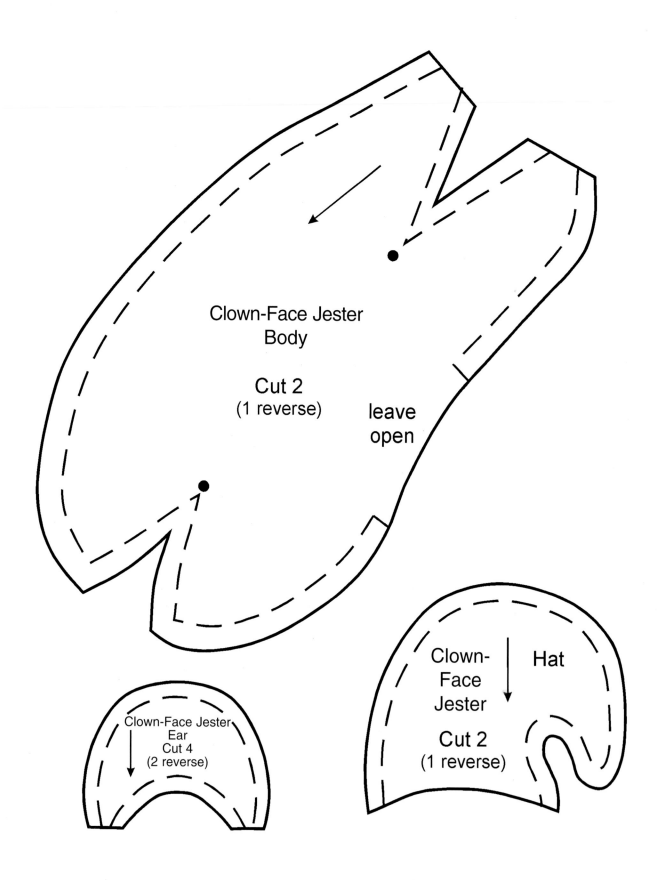

Clown-Face Jester
Body

Cut 2
(1 reverse)

leave
open

Clown-Face Jester
Ear
Cut 4
(2 reverse)

Clown-
Face
Jester

Hat

Cut 2
(1 reverse)

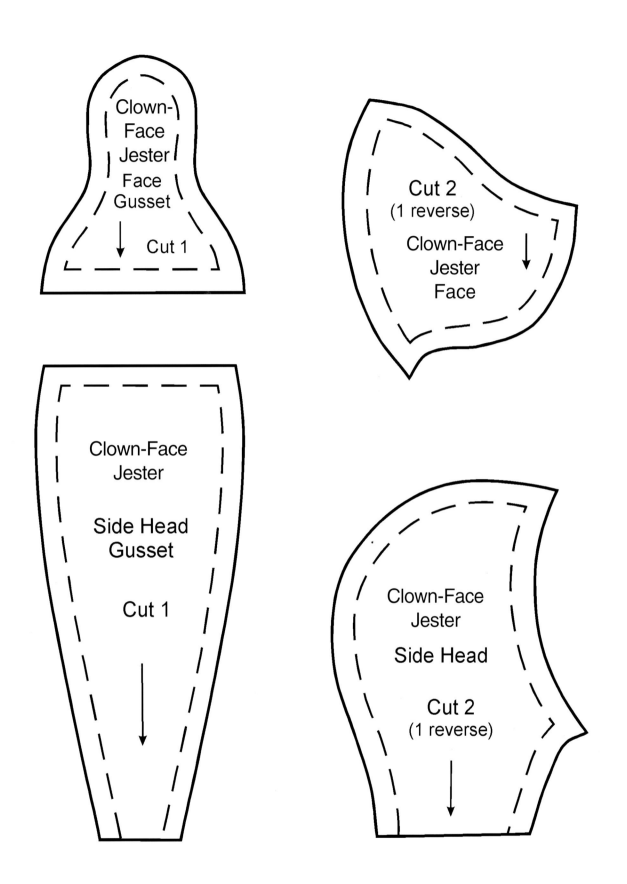

Clown-Face
Jester
Face
Gusset

Cut 1

Cut 2
(1 reverse)

Clown-Face
Jester
Face

Clown-Face
Jester

Side Head
Gusset

Cut 1

Clown-Face
Jester

Side Head

Cut 2
(1 reverse)

Roosevelt

(Size: 17 inches; Difficulty Level: 8)

MATERIALS

- ☐ One piece 10" x 18" gold mohair, 1/2" pile, for head and paws
- ☐ 1/2 yard dark-green mohair, 1/8" pile, or 1/2 yard vintage wool army blanket
- ☐ 1/4 yard brown leatherette fabric for boots and belts
- ☐ One 9" x 9" gold 100% wool felt for paws
- ☐ One pair of commercial eyeglasses
- ☐ One red kerchief for scarf
- ☐ 4 flat gold buttons for jacket
- ☐ One small belt buckle
- ☐ One pair 6mm glass or plastic eyes
- ☐ Five 1½" joint sets
- ☐ #3 black pearl cotton thread
- ☐ Sewing-machine thread for seams, color to match fabric
- ☐ Polyester fiberfill for stuffing (optional excelsior stuffing for a vintage look)
- ☐ Nylon upholstery thread for seams, color to match mohair

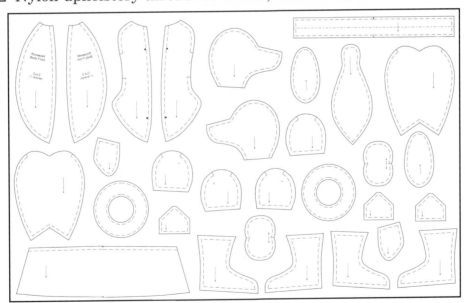

This diagram represents all of the pattern pieces required to complete this bear, laid out in the straight of the fabric. More than one piece of fabric may be required for laying out the pattern pieces.

INSTRUCTIONS

1

Sew two side heads from nose down to neck edge.

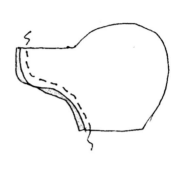

2

Sew head gusset to the side head section.

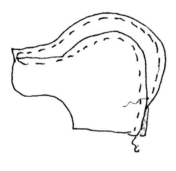

3

Fold ear and sew, twice. Clip the center of the ear for turning.

cut and
leave open

4

Sew one mohair and one felt paw to each arm for both right and left arms. Make sure the felt paw is on the inside of the arm.

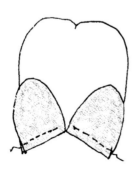

5

Fold arm and sew, leaving the top open for stuffing.

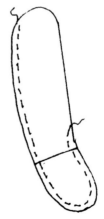

6

Sew upper leg to boot for both right and left legs.

7

Put two leg sections together and sew, leaving the top open for stuffing, for both right and left legs.

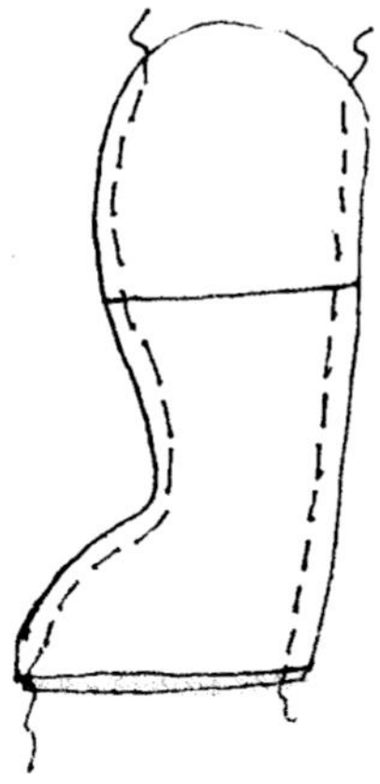

8

Baste sole to bottom of boot, then machine-sew both right and left boots.

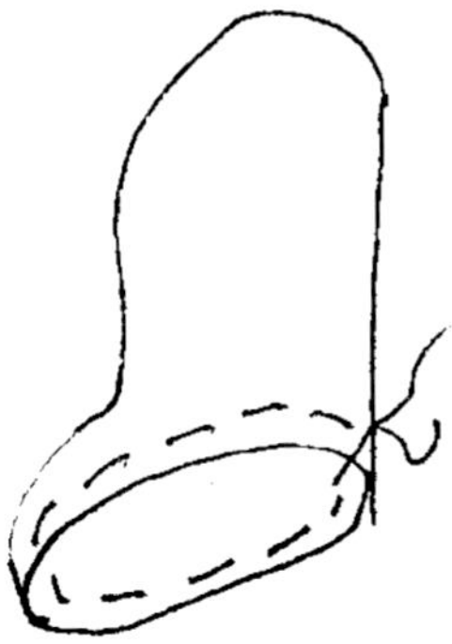

9

Sew center body front seams together.

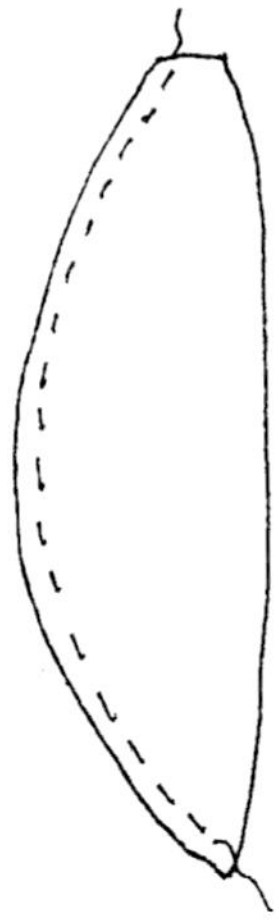

10

Sew body back seams together, leaving the center open for stuffing.

11

Sew front and back body sections together at side seams.

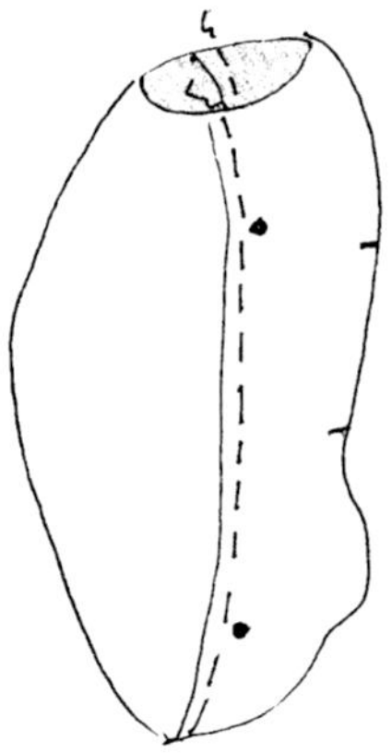

12

Stuff head and attach to body. Attach arms and legs. Stuff body, arms and legs, and close. Sew three hat crown pieces together to form the top of the hat.

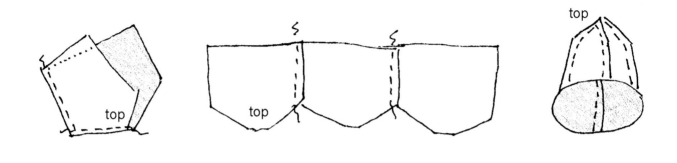

13

Sew two hat brim pieces together, turn inside out and top-stitch.

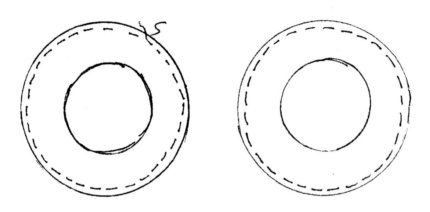

14

Sew brim to crown, then zig-zag stitch the seam.

Sew band to jacket skirt top.

15

16

Sew band to right side, top-stitch.

Attach belt buckle to jacket band (look at a real belt to see how it's done). Attach jacket skirt to finished bear at waist over the front center seam of the body.

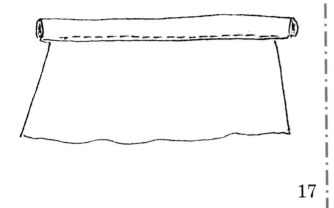

17

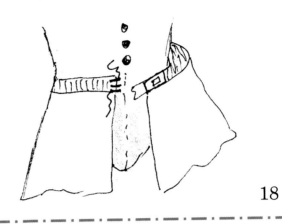

18

Sew the other side of jacket skirt with buckle over the left attachment.

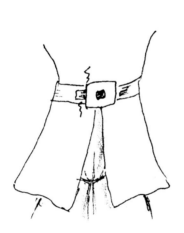

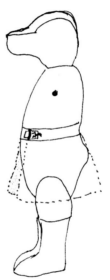

19

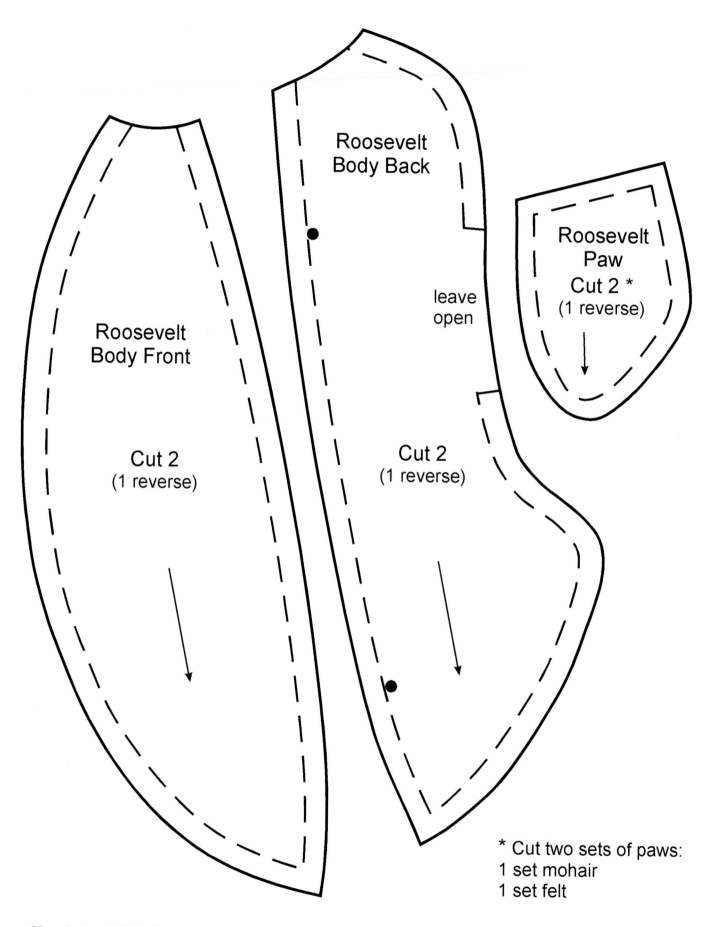

Roosevelt
Body Back

Roosevelt
Paw
Cut 2 *
(1 reverse)

leave
open

Roosevelt
Body Front

Cut 2
(1 reverse)

Cut 2
(1 reverse)

* Cut two sets of paws:
1 set mohair
1 set felt

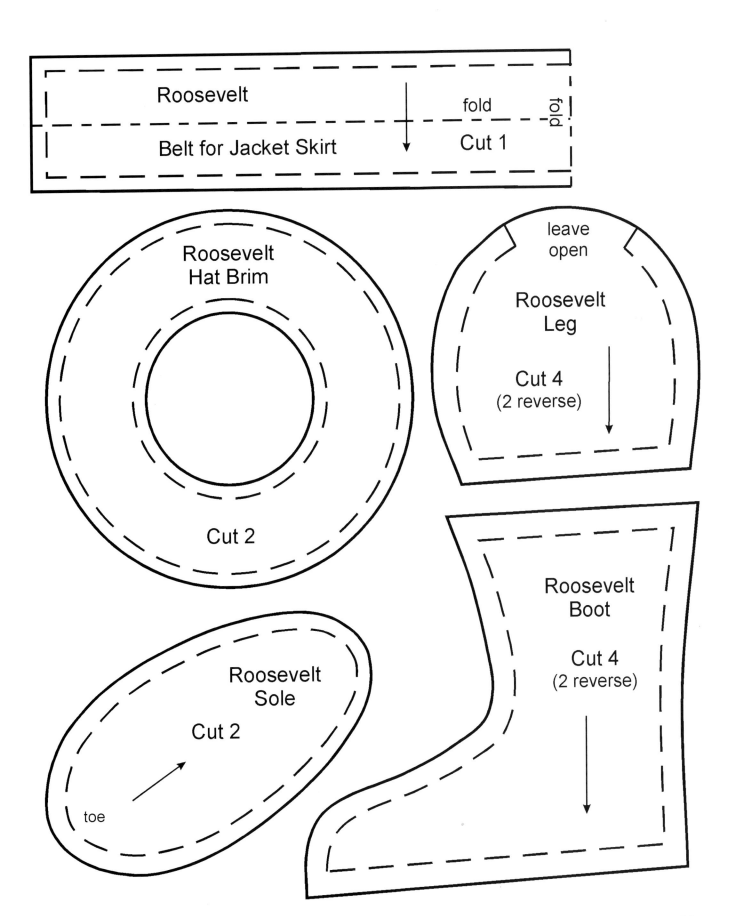

Roosevelt

Belt for Jacket Skirt

fold

fold

Cut 1

Roosevelt
Hat Brim

Cut 2

leave
open

Roosevelt
Leg

Cut 4
(2 reverse)

Roosevelt
Sole

Cut 2

toe

Roosevelt
Boot

Cut 4
(2 reverse)

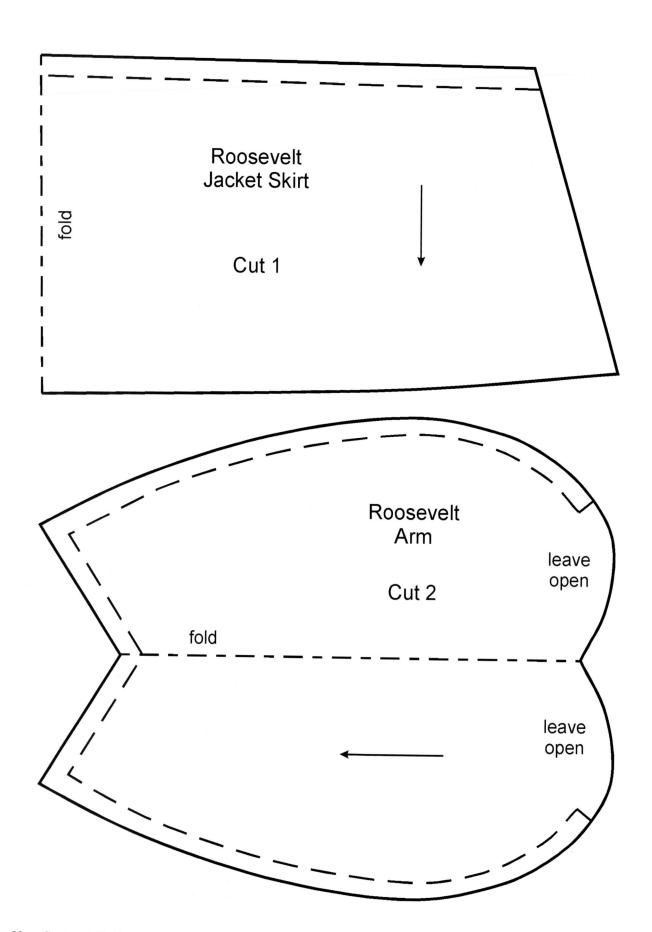

Roosevelt
Jacket Skirt

fold

Cut 1

Roosevelt
Arm

leave
open

Cut 2

fold

leave
open

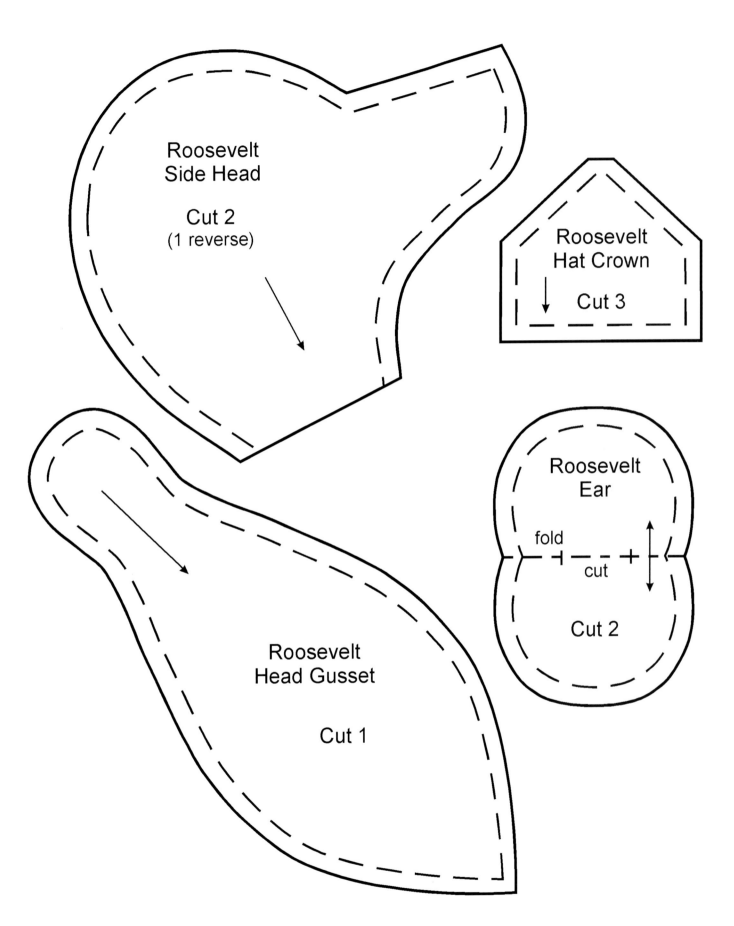

Roosevelt
Side Head

Cut 2
(1 reverse)

Roosevelt
Hat Crown

Cut 3

Roosevelt
Ear

fold

cut

Cut 2

Roosevelt
Head Gusset

Cut 1

Pajama Bear

(Size: 13 inches; Difficulty Level: 9)

MATERIALS

- ☐ 1/4 yards each of white and gold mohair, 1/4" pile
- ☐ One 9" x 9" beige 100% wool felt for paws
- ☐ One 2" x 20" of white ribbed cotton for cuffs on arms and body
- ☐ One pair 6mm glass or plastic eyes
- ☐ Five 1/2" joint sets
- ☐ #5 black pearl cotton for nose and mouth
- ☐ Sewing-machine thread for seams, color to match fabric
- ☐ Polyester fiberfill for stuffing (optional excelsior stuffing for the vintage look)
- ☐ Nylon upholstery thread for attaching eyes and closing
- ☐ 4 colors acrylic paint for creating confetti look

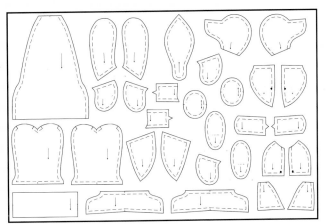

This diagram represents all of the pattern pieces required to complete this bear, laid out in the straight of the fabric. More than one piece of fabric may be required for laying out the pattern pieces.

INSTRUCTIONS

1

Before starting to sew this bear, paint multi-colored dots on the BACK of the fabric.

Using the paint from the tube, dip the rounded tip of a brush HANDLE into the paint and press firmly onto the mohair backing of the top and bottom sections of the body front and back.

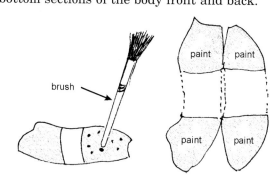

2

Sew two side head pieces together from nose to neck edge.

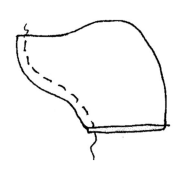

3

Sew center head gusset to side head section.

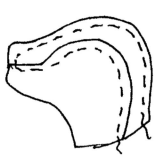

4

Sew two ear pieces together, twice.

5

Sew ribbing piece to bottom arm.

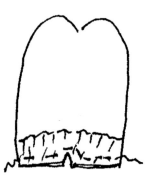

6

Sew one mohair and one felt paw to each arm for both right and left arms. Make sure the felt paw is on the inside of the arm.

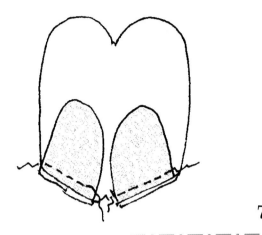

7

Fold arm in half and sew, leaving the top open for stuffing.

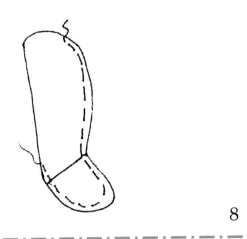

8

Sew ribbing to bottom of both right and left legs.

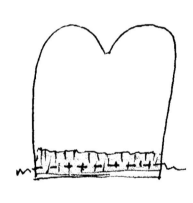

9

Sew foot to leg on both legs.

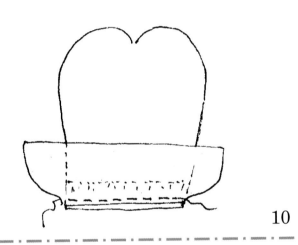

10

Fold leg and sew, leaving the top open for stuffing.

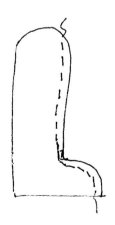

11

Baste sole to the bottom of the leg, then machine-stitch.

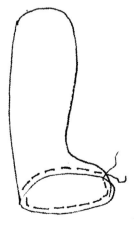

12

Sew front body top to front body middle. Sew front body middle to front body bottom. Sew back body top to back body middle. Sew back body middle to back bottom.

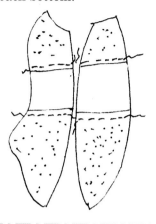

13

Sew back and front sections together at front and back side seams, leaving the center back open for stuffing. Stuff head and attach to body. Attach arms and legs. Stuff body, arms, legs, and close. Hand-sew the ribbing around the top upper body.

attach ribbing

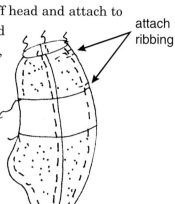

14

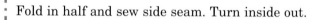

Sew ribbing to bottom edge of hat piece.

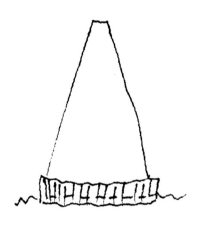

15

Fold in half and sew side seam. Turn inside out.

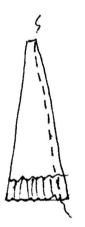

16

Make a pompom. Cut two cardboard disks, 1½" diameter with a hole in the middle. With both disks together, thread yarn through the hole, then around disk and back through the hole. Continue until the entire disk is covered. Cut the yarn around the outside perimeter of the disks. Separate the disks slightly, insert a piece of yarn and tie the bundle of yarn together tightly. Carefully remove the cardboard disks and fluff up the pompom. Attach to the top of the hat.

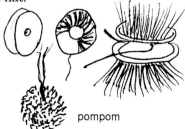

pompom

17

Attach hat to head.

18

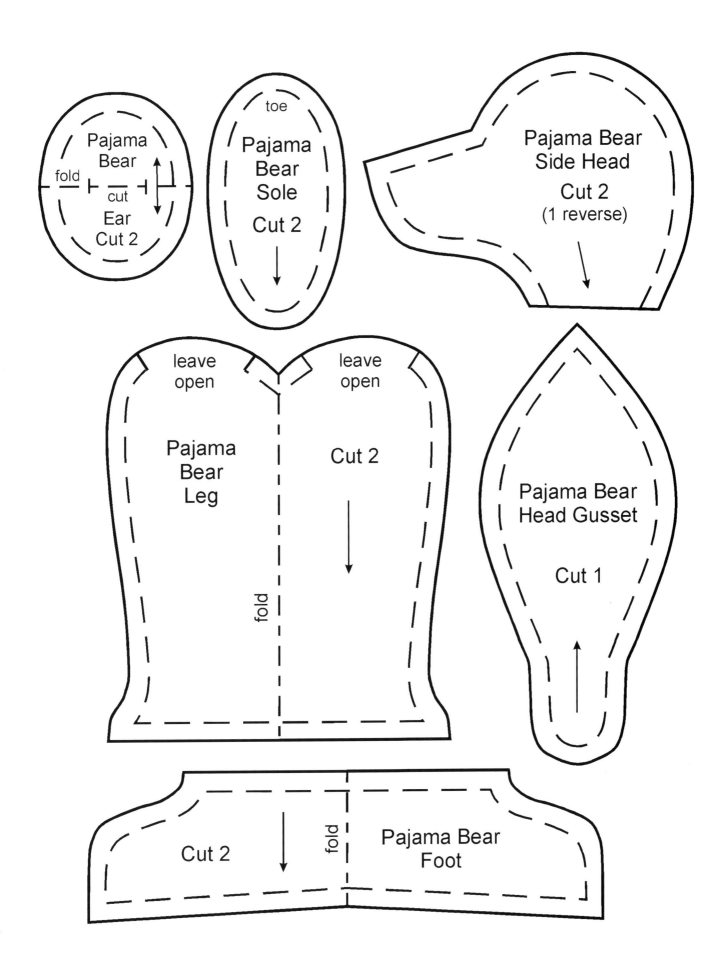

Pajama Bear
Ear
Cut 2
fold
cut

Pajama Bear
Sole
Cut 2
toe

Pajama Bear
Side Head
Cut 2
(1 reverse)

Pajama Bear
Leg
leave open
leave open
Cut 2
fold

Pajama Bear
Head Gusset
Cut 1

Pajama Bear
Foot
Cut 2
fold

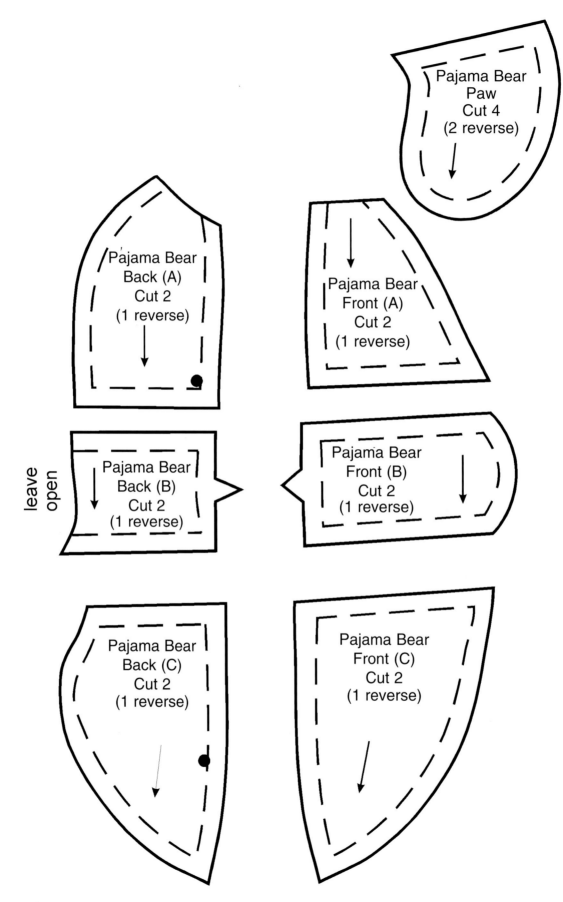

Pajama Bear
Paw
Cut 4
(2 reverse)

Pajama Bear
Back (A)
Cut 2
(1 reverse)

Pajama Bear
Front (A)
Cut 2
(1 reverse)

leave
open

Pajama Bear
Back (B)
Cut 2
(1 reverse)

Pajama Bear
Front (B)
Cut 2
(1 reverse)

Pajama Bear
Back (C)
Cut 2
(1 reverse)

Pajama Bear
Front (C)
Cut 2
(1 reverse)

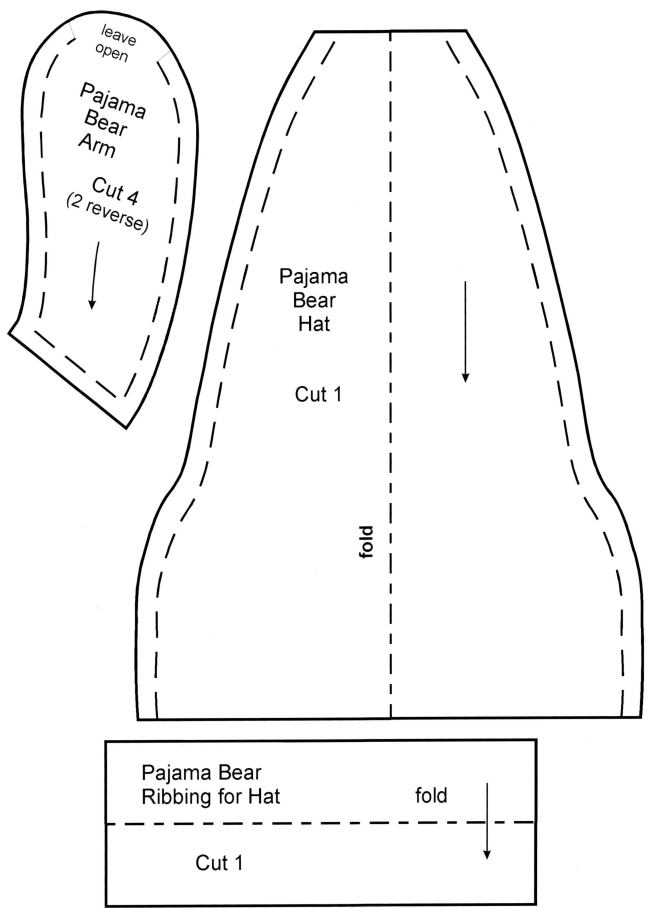

leave
open

Pajama
Bear
Arm

Cut 4
(2 reverse)

Pajama
Bear
Hat

Cut 1

fold

Pajama Bear
Ribbing for Hat

fold

Cut 1

Chef Chris

(Size: 23 inches; Difficulty Level: 10)

MATERIALS

- ☐ 3/4 yard gold mohair, 1/2" pile
- ☐ One piece 9" x 9" upholstery or felt fabric for paws, soles, mouth.
- ☐ One piece 5" x 10" beige mohair, 2" pile, for face muzzle
- ☐ One pair of 8mm glass or plastic eyes
- ☐ Five 2" joint sets
- ☐ #3 brown pearl cotton for nose
- ☐ Sewing-machine thread for seams, color to match fabric
- ☐ Waxed thread for attaching eyes
- ☐ Nylon thread for closing seams
- ☐ Polyester fiberfill for stuffing
- ☐ 1/2 yard white medium weight fabric for jacket and hat
- ☐ Eight 3/8" buttons for jacket

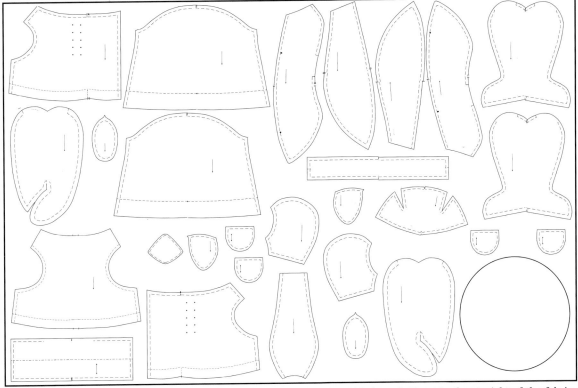

This diagram represents all of the pattern pieces required to complete this bear, laid out in the straight of the fabric. More than one piece of fabric may be required for laying out the pattern pieces.

INSTRUCTIONS

1

Sew side head to center head gusset on both sides.

2

Sew muzzle to side head and gusset section.

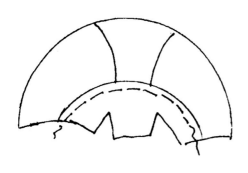

3

Fold head in half and sew A to B and C to D on muzzle. Leave the mouth area open.

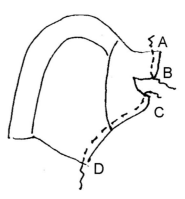

4

Position the mouth gusset to correspond to the mouth opening on the muzzle (A, B, C). Pin mouth gusset into muzzle, hand baste in, then machine stitch.

5

Sew two body fronts and two body backs together at front and back center seams. Leave center back open for stuffing. Sew front and back of body together at side seams.

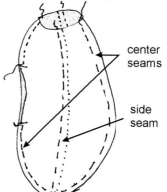

center
seams

side
seam

6

Sew two ears together, twice.

7

Fold leg in half and sew together, leaving the top open for stuffing. Baste the sole to the bottom of the leg then machine-sew the sole to the leg.

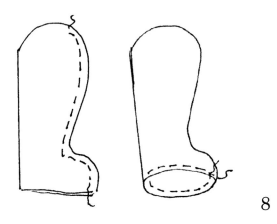

8

Sew paws to inner arms, both right and left sides.

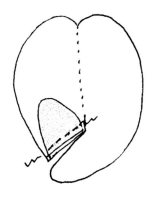

9

Fold arms in half and sew together, leaving open the top for stuffing.

Refer to the Basic Directions to complete the head and attach the head, arms, and legs to the body. Stuff and close the open seams.

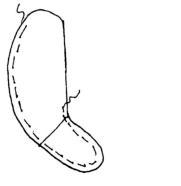

10

Pin jacket front to jacket back at shoulder and side seams, right sides together, and sew along shoulder and side seams.

back

11

Hem edge of jacket front facing. Fold facing and sew to front jacket neck edge.

12

Fold sleeve in half and sew side seam.

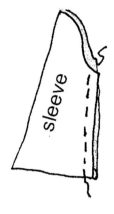

13

Place sleeve in arm hole and sew from inside jacket.

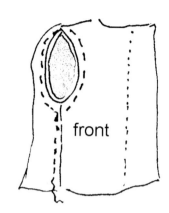

14

Fold collar in half and sew side edges. Turn inside out.

15

Attach collar about 1½" from edge of jacket and sew one edge of collar to jacket neck. Fold facing edge 1/4" and top stitch. Fold facing (wrong sides together) and sew 1½" seam.

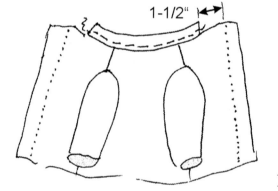

16

Sew buttons to front of jacket and sew snaps to the inside of jacket (no button holes needed).

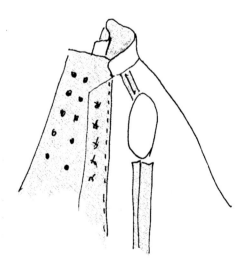

17

Gather hat crown piece to fit the band.

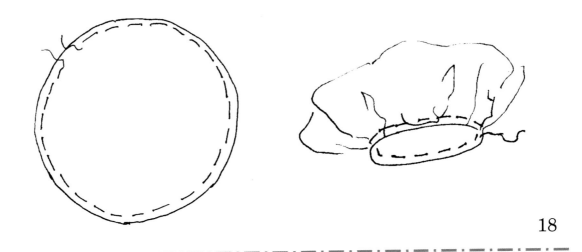

18

Sew hat band together and sew to the crown edge.

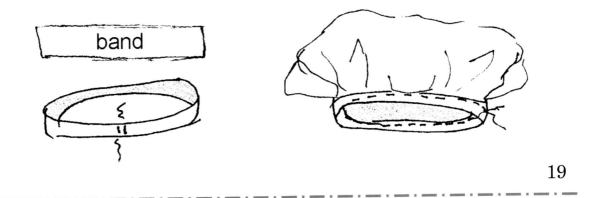

band

19

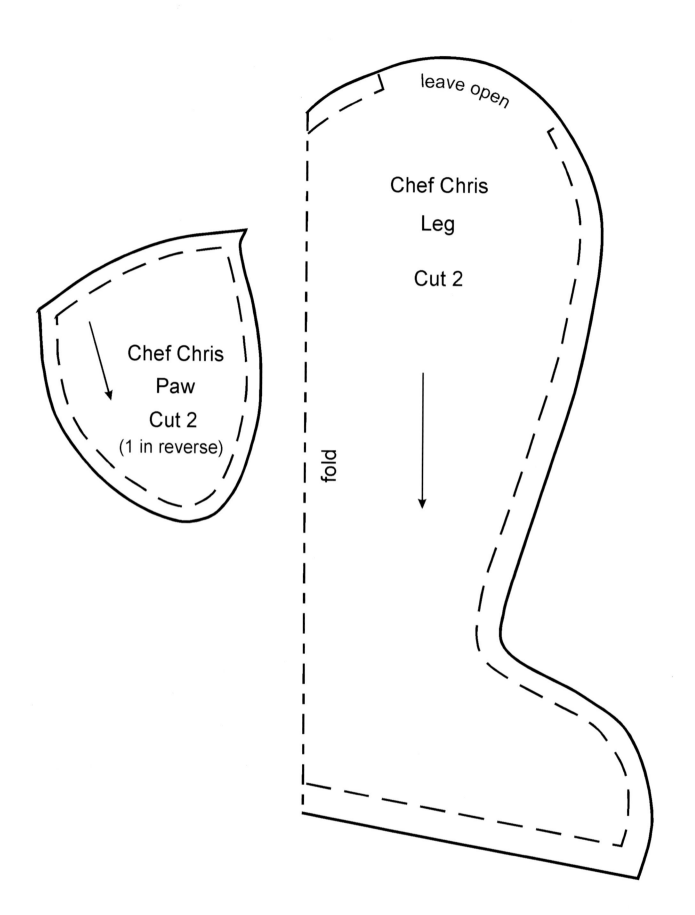

leave open

Chef Chris

Leg

Cut 2

Chef Chris

Paw

Cut 2

(1 in reverse)

fold

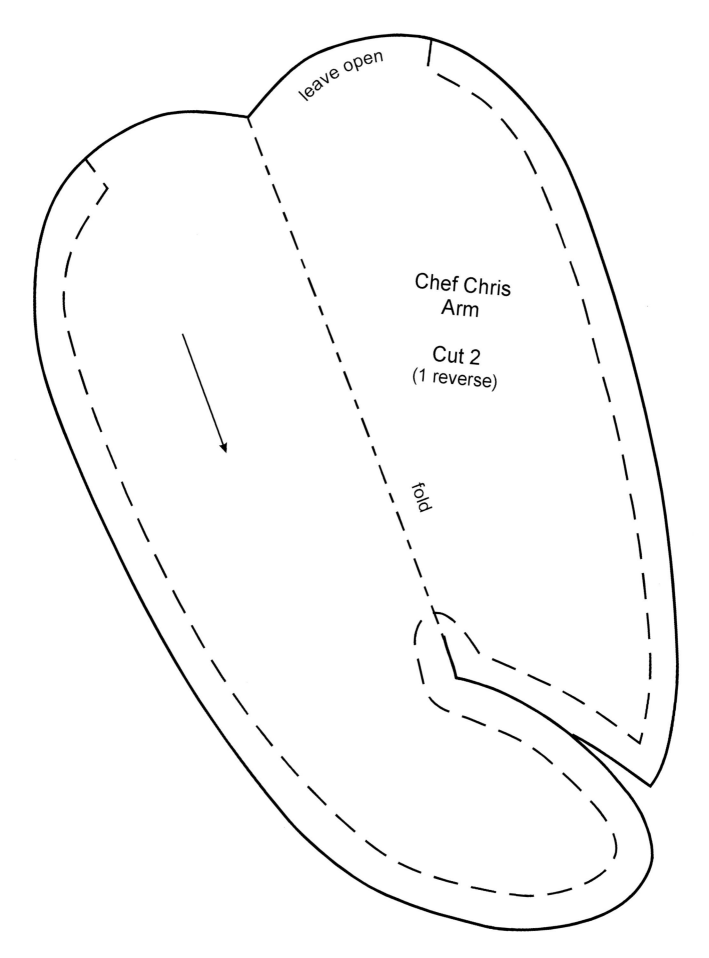

leave open

Chef Chris
Arm

Cut 2
(1 reverse)

fold

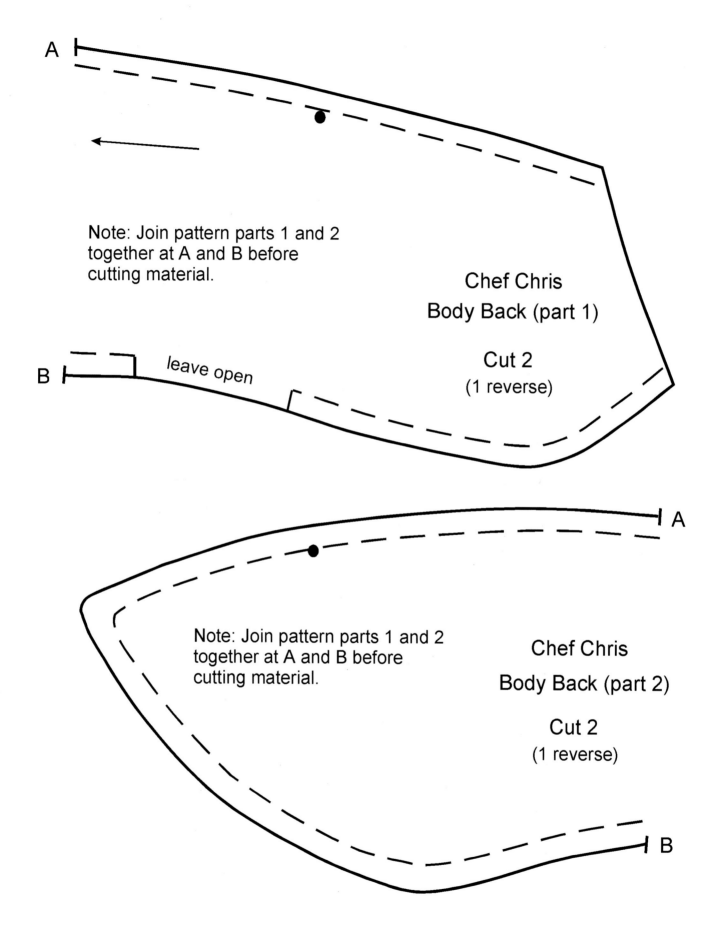

A

Note: Join pattern parts 1 and 2
together at A and B before
cutting material.

B

leave open

Chef Chris
Body Back (part 1)

Cut 2
(1 reverse)

A

Note: Join pattern parts 1 and 2
together at A and B before
cutting material.

Chef Chris
Body Back (part 2)

Cut 2
(1 reverse)

B

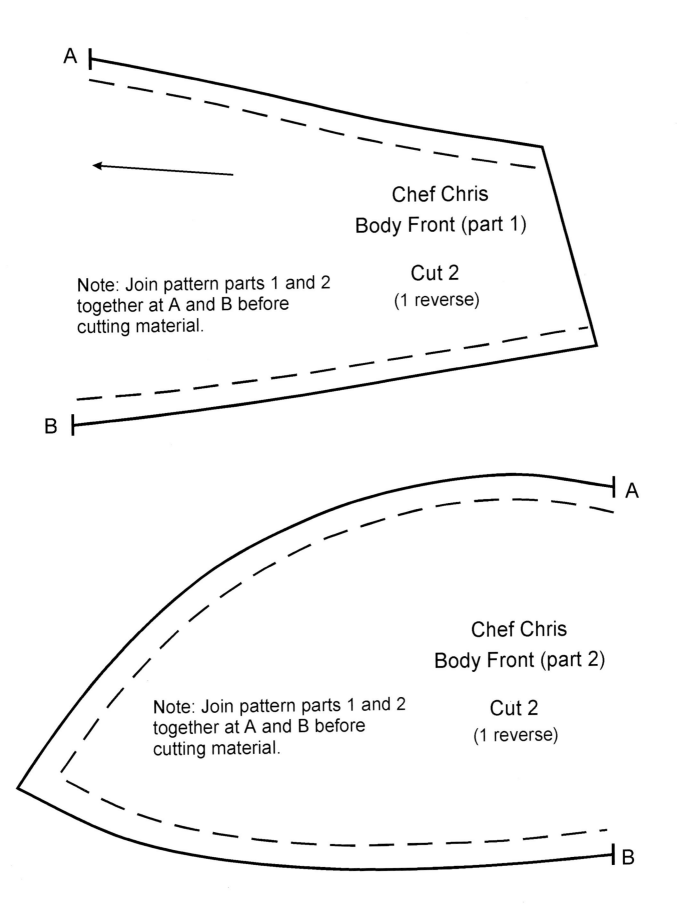

A

Chef Chris
Body Front (part 1)

Cut 2
(1 reverse)

Note: Join pattern parts 1 and 2
together at A and B before
cutting material.

B

Chef Chris
Body Front (part 2)

Cut 2
(1 reverse)

Note: Join pattern parts 1 and 2
together at A and B before
cutting material.

A

B

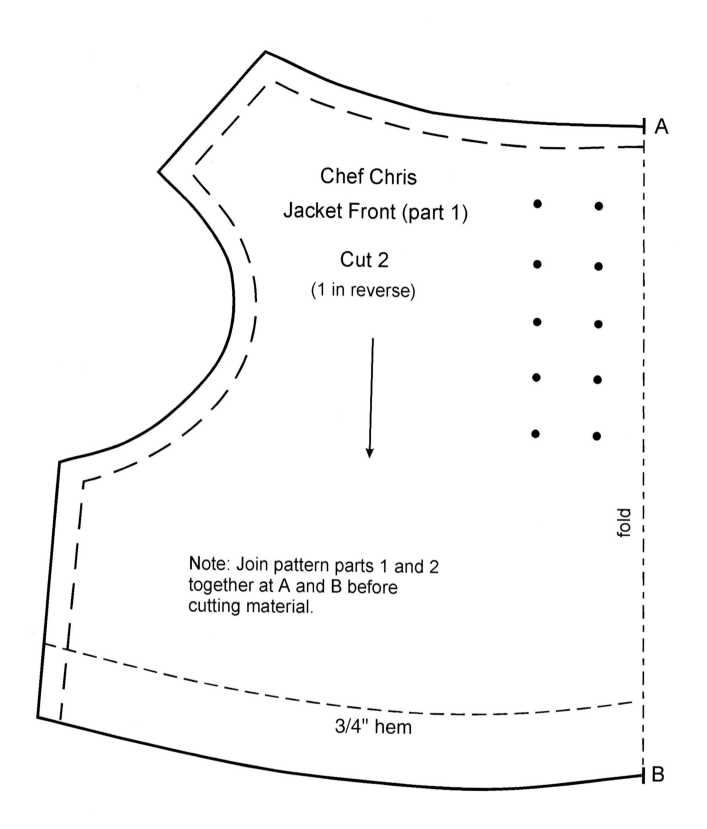

Chef Chris
Jacket Front (part 1)

Cut 2
(1 in reverse)

A

fold

Note: Join pattern parts 1 and 2
together at A and B before
cutting material.

3/4" hem

B

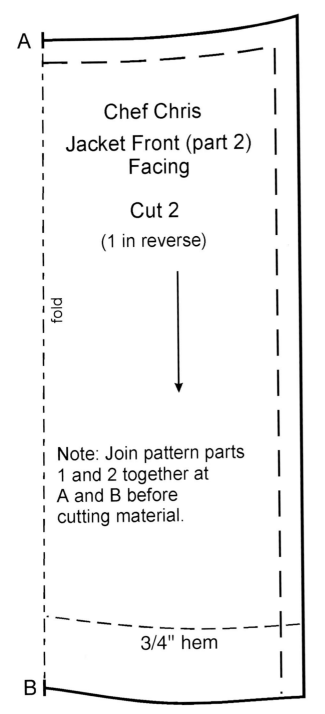

A

Chef Chris
Jacket Front (part 2)
Facing

Cut 2

(1 in reverse)

fold

Note: Join pattern parts
1 and 2 together at
A and B before
cutting material.

3/4" hem

B

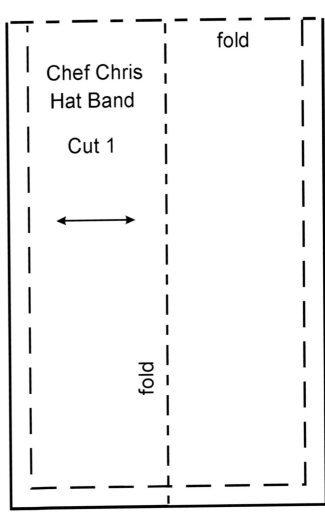

Chef Chris
Hat Band

Cut 1

fold

fold

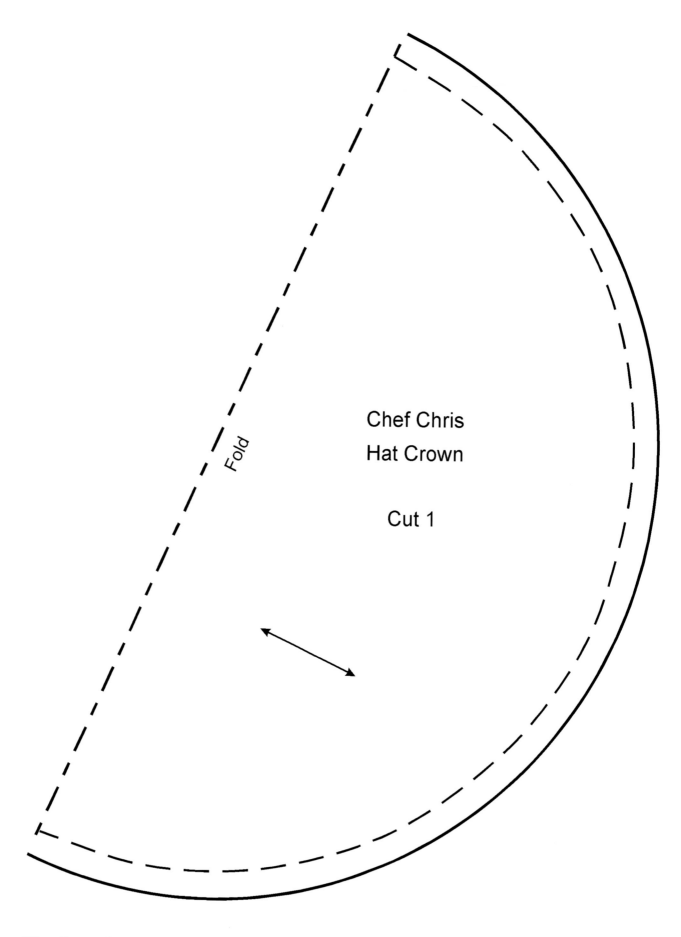

Fold

Chef Chris
Hat Crown

Cut 1

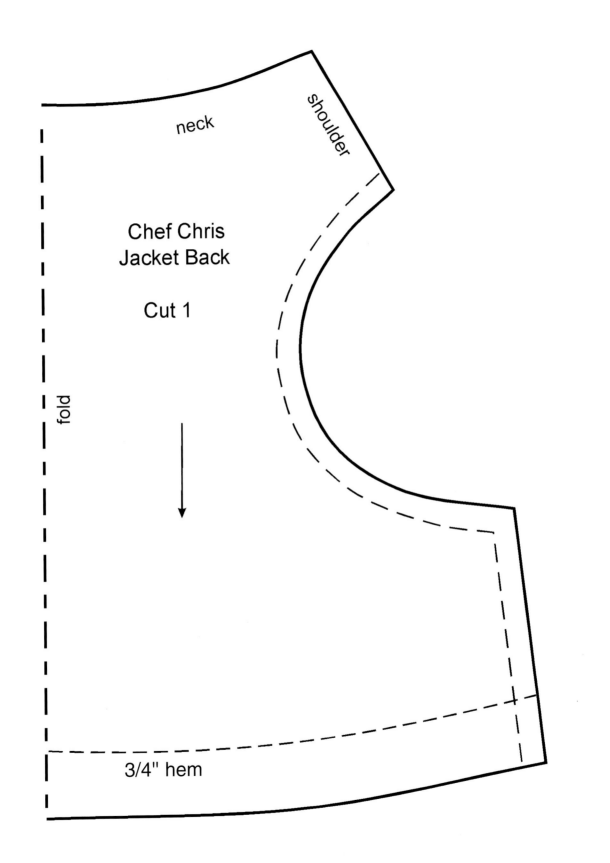

neck

shoulder

Chef Chris
Jacket Back

Cut 1

fold

3/4" hem

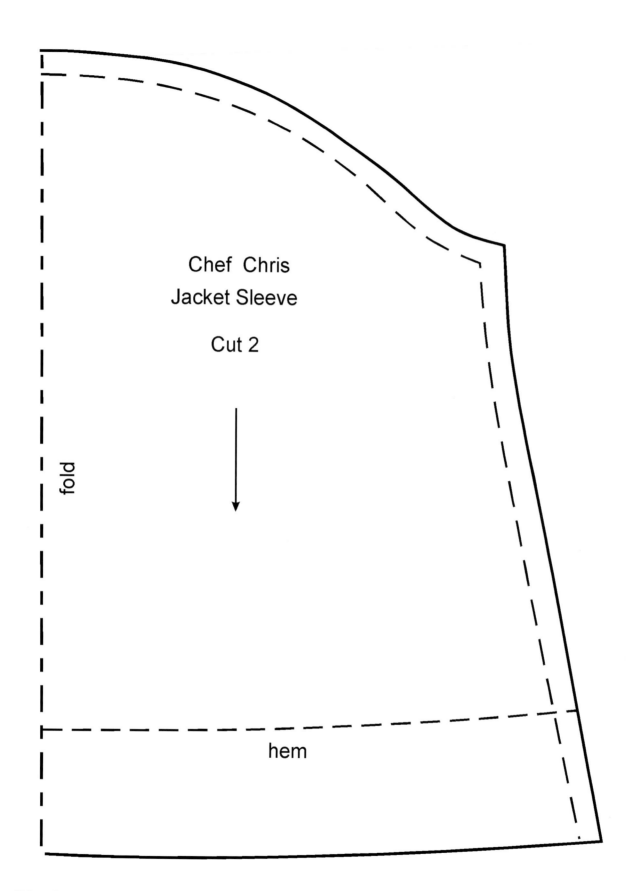

Chef Chris
Jacket Sleeve

Cut 2

fold

hem

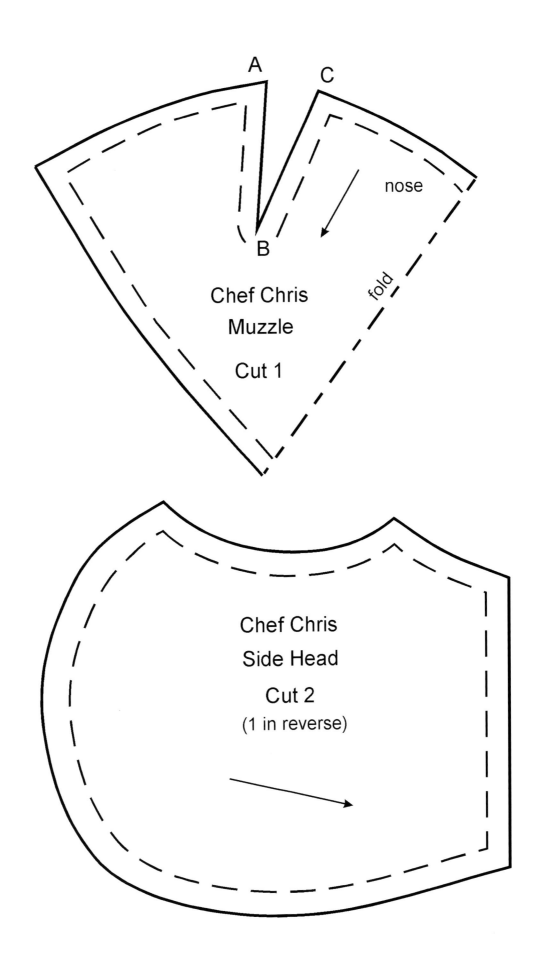

A

C

nose

B

fold

Chef Chris

Muzzle

Cut 1

Chef Chris

Side Head

Cut 2

(1 in reverse)

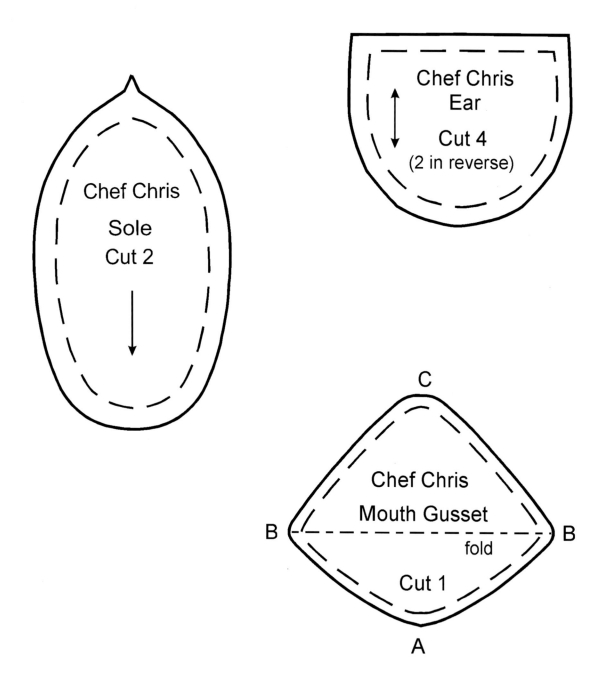

Chef Chris

Sole
Cut 2

Chef Chris
Ear

Cut 4
(2 in reverse)

C

Chef Chris

Mouth Gusset

B   fold   B

Cut 1

A

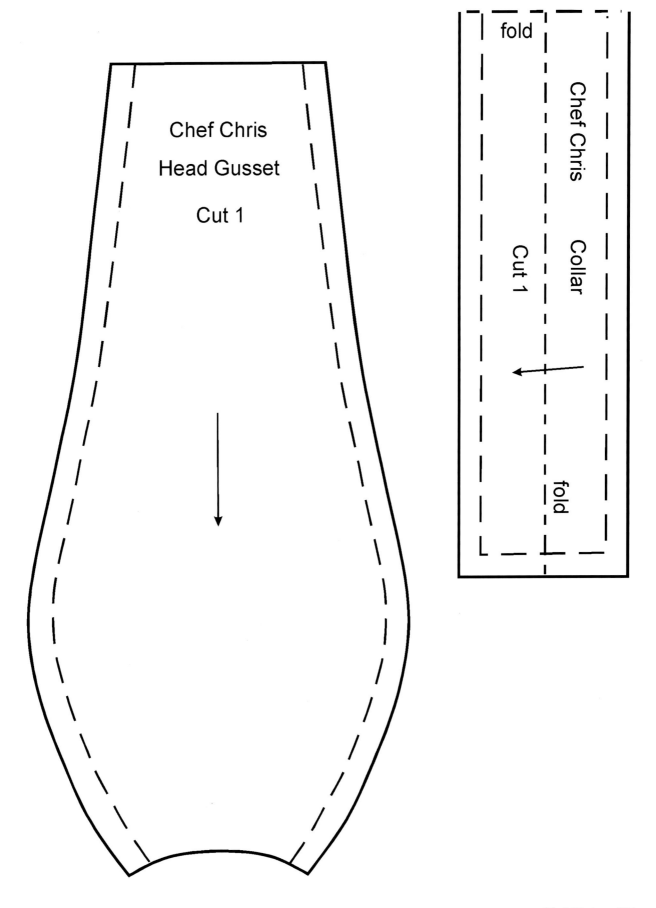

Chef Chris
Head Gusset
Cut 1

Chef Chris   Collar

Cut 1

fold

fold

Punky

(Size: 19 inches; Difficulty Level: 11)

MATERIALS

- ☐ 1/4 yard pink mohair, 1/2" pile, for lower body and upper legs
- ☐ 1/4 yard light-green mohair, 1/2" pile, for upper body and upper arms
- ☐ One piece 6" x 20" turquoise mohair, 1/2" pile, for lower arms
- ☐ One piece 8" x 8" purple mohair, 1/2" pile, for lower legs
- ☐ One piece 9" x 4" lavender mohair, 1/2" pile, for feet
- ☐ One piece 9" x 13" white string mohair, 1" pile, for head and paws and ears
- ☐ One piece 6½" x 5" white upholstery fabric for inner paws
- ☐ One piece 3" x 10" dark-green upholstery fabric for upper and lower arm gusset
- ☐ One piece 3" x 10" light-purple upholstery fabric for upper and lower leg gusset
- ☐ One pair 8mm black glass eyes
- ☐ #5 turquoise pearl cotton
- ☐ #5 black pearl cotton for mouth and paws
- ☐ Five 1½" joint sets
- ☐ One small tube purple acrylic paint for the top of the head (Mohawk hairdo)
- ☐ Sixteen 3/8" gold buttons for attaching arms, legs, paws, feet
- ☐ Sewing-machine thread for seams, colors to match fabric
- ☐ Nylon thread for closing seams
- ☐ Polyester fiberfill and plastic or glass beads for stuffing (The beads give the bear weight so it will sit better.)

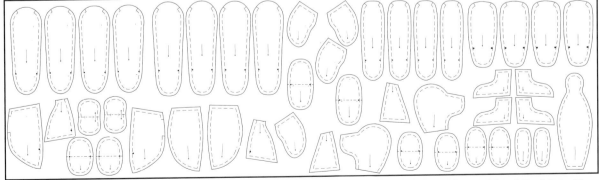

This diagram represents all of the pattern pieces required to complete this bear, laid out in the straight of the fabric. More than one piece of fabric may be required for laying out the pattern pieces.

INSTRUCTIONS

1

Sew two side heads together from nose to neck edge.

2

Sew head gusset to side head pieces.

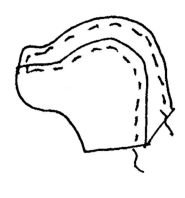

3

Sew two sets of upper arms, leaving open at gusset markings. Leave top open for stuffing.

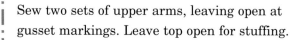

A B

4

Sew two sets of lower arms, leaving open at gusset markings. Leave top open for stuffing.

C D

5

Sew mohair and upholstery paw pieces together, right and left paws.

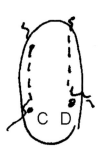

6

Open upper and lower arms and sew in gussets.

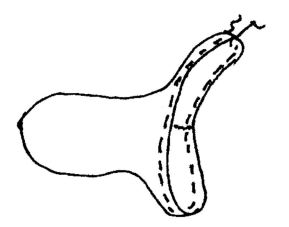

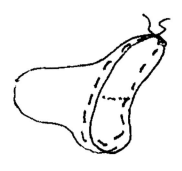

7

Sew the upper and lower legs in the same way as the arms.

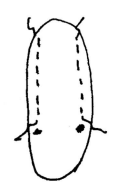 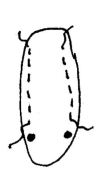

8

Sew two sets of shoes. On each shoe, baste the sole into the bottom of the shoe, then machine-sew the sole to the shoe.

9

Sew body front top and front bottom together. Sew body back top and back bottom together.

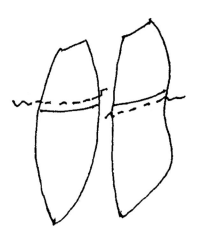

10

Sew front and back sections together, leaving center back open for stuffing. Sew side seams together.

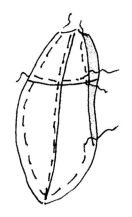

11

Stuff all sections of arms and legs from top of piece. DO NOT stuff the gusset area.

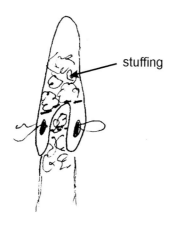

stuffing

12

Attach arms and legs at gusset area with the gold buttons.

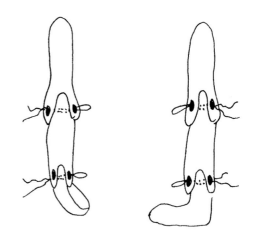

13

Fold ear and sew, cutting a center section on fold to turn inside out. Attach to head.

cut and leave open

14

Paint a purple center strip on top of the head, in the style of a mohawk hairdo.

15

Finish head before attaching it to the body. Gather neck edge on head and insert fender washer, fiber disk and T-cotter pin, then close. Attach eyes and embroider nose and mouth on face.

16

Attach head, arms and legs to body with T-cotter pin joints.

Stuff body with plastic or glass beads and polyester fiberfill. Close with ladder stitch.

Remember to double-stitch seams on pieces that are filled with pellets.

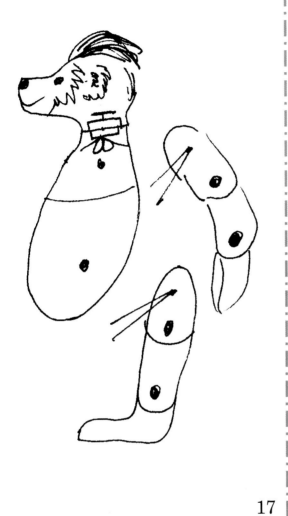

17

18

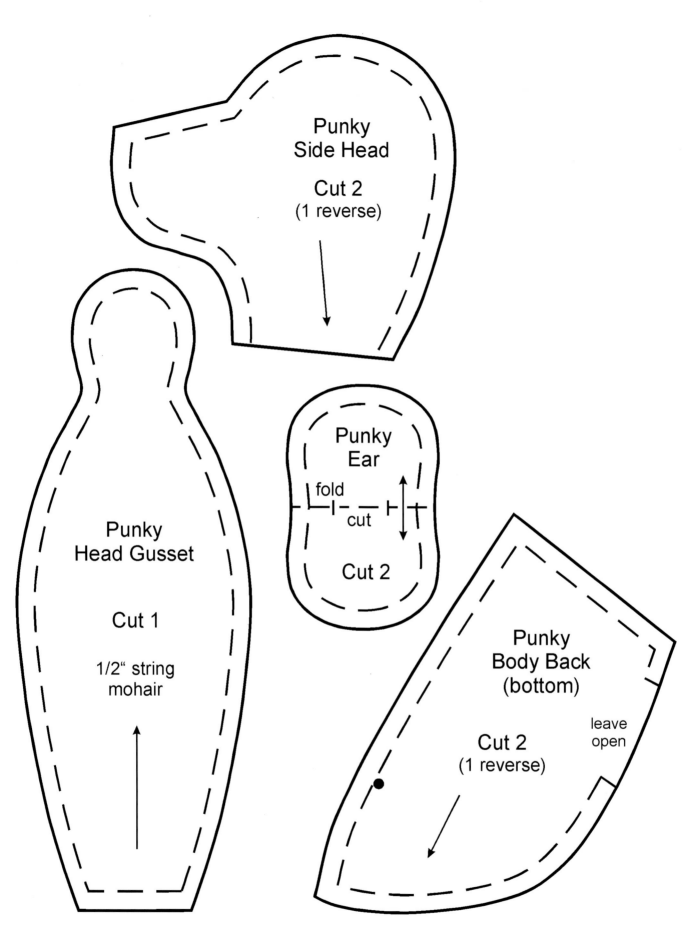

Punky
Side Head

Cut 2
(1 reverse)

Punky
Head Gusset

Cut 1

1/2" string
mohair

Punky
Ear

fold

cut

Cut 2

Punky
Body Back
(bottom)

leave
open

Cut 2
(1 reverse)

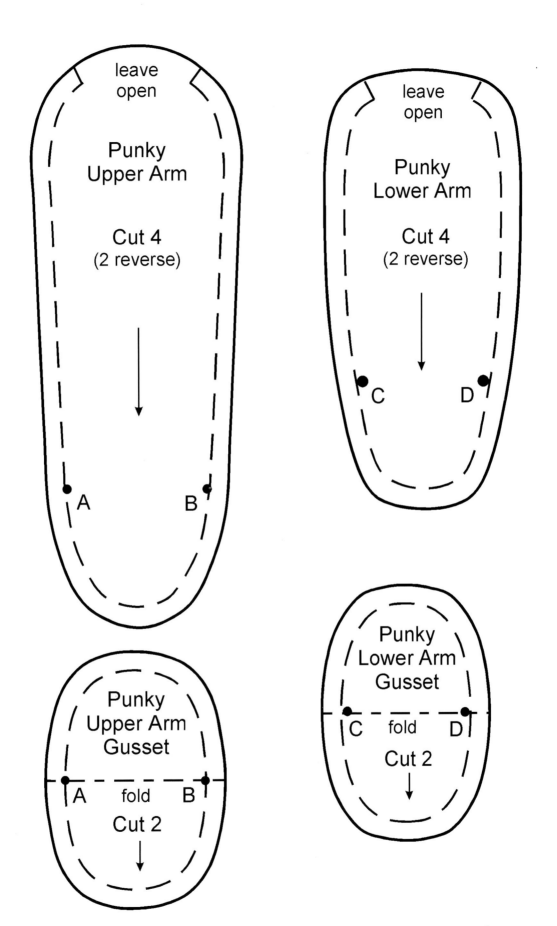

leave open

Punky
Upper Arm

Cut 4
(2 reverse)

A   B

leave open

Punky
Lower Arm

Cut 4
(2 reverse)

C   D

Punky
Upper Arm
Gusset

A   fold   B

Cut 2

Punky
Lower Arm
Gusset

C   fold   D

Cut 2

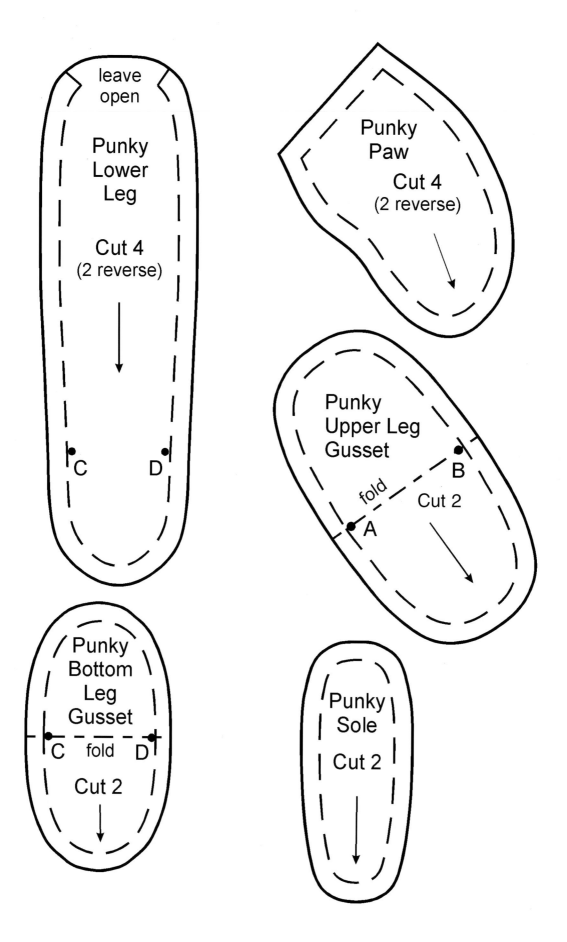

leave
open

Punky
Lower
Leg

Cut 4
(2 reverse)

C   D

Punky
Paw

Cut 4
(2 reverse)

Punky
Upper Leg
Gusset

fold

B

Cut 2

A

Punky
Bottom
Leg
Gusset

C   fold   D

Cut 2

Punky
Sole

Cut 2

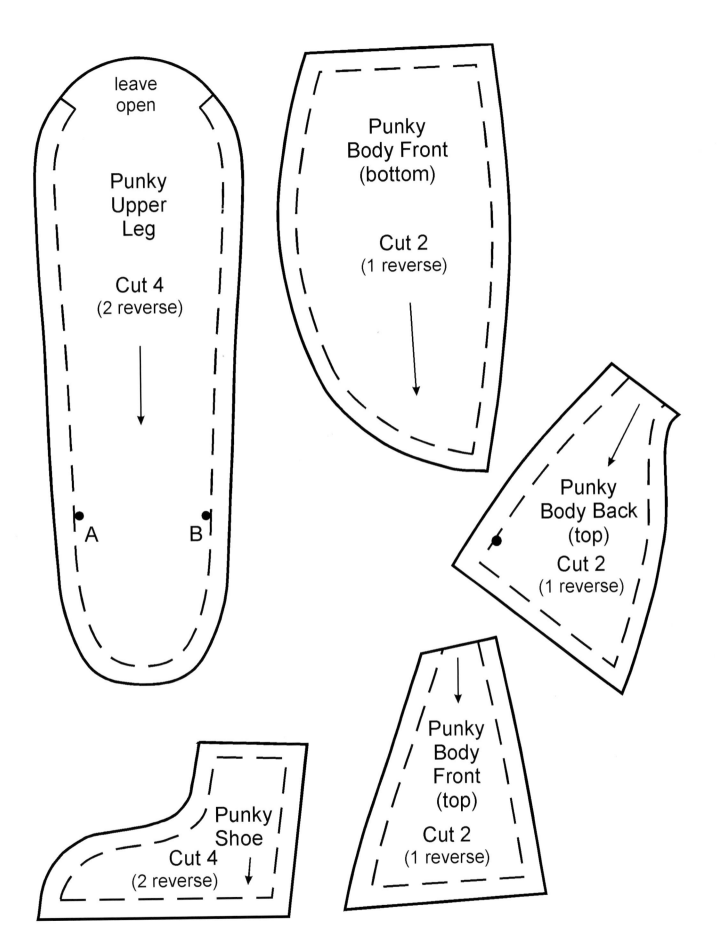

leave
open

Punky
Upper
Leg

Cut 4
(2 reverse)

A B

Punky
Body Front
(bottom)

Cut 2
(1 reverse)

Punky
Body Back
(top)
Cut 2
(1 reverse)

Punky
Shoe
Cut 4
(2 reverse)

Punky
Body
Front
(top)
Cut 2
(1 reverse)

Mr. Farmer

(Size: 14 inches; Difficulty Level: 12)

MATERIALS

- ☐ One piece 24" x 12" brown upholstery fabric for head, arms and feet
- ☐ One piece 9" x 22" jeans fabric
- ☐ One piece 9" x 15" plaid print upholstery fabric for shirt
- ☐ Small piece 2" x 13" kerchief fabric
- ☐ One strip 1/2" width leather for suspenders
- ☐ Four 3/8" buttons for attaching suspenders
- ☐ Eight 3/8" buttons for shirt front
- ☐ One small straw hat
- ☐ One pair 7mm glass eyes or plastic eyes
- ☐ Three 1" T-cotter pin joint sets
- ☐ #5 black pearl cotton for nose and mouth
- ☐ Small piece of beeswax for waxing the nose
- ☐ Sewing-machine thread for seams, color to match fabric
- ☐ Waxed thread for attaching eyes
- ☐ Nylon upholstery thread for closing seams
- ☐ Polyester fiberfill for stuffing

This diagram represents all of the pattern pieces required to complete this bear, laid out in the straight of the fabric. More than one piece of fabric may be required for laying out the pattern pieces.

INSTRUCTIONS

Sew both side heads to center head gusset.

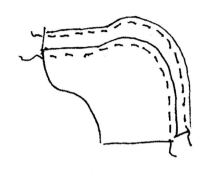

1

2

Fold center gusset so side heads match and stitch side heads from the center nose down to the neck.

Fold ear in half and stitch. Cut in center of fold to turn.

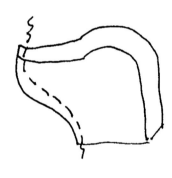

cut and leave open

3

4

Sew upper arm to lower arm. Sew two arms pieces together, twice.

Sew top of body to bottom of body. Sew center front of body together.

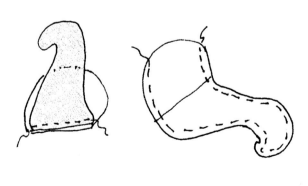

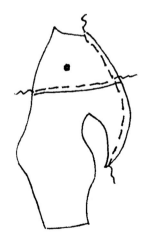

5

6

Sew foot to the bottom of leg.

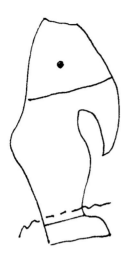

7

Sew inner leg to outer leg.

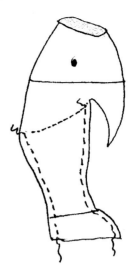

8

Sew lower body B to crotch B around the inner leg opening. Sew sole to foot.

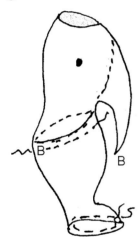

9

Finish the body by sewing from B to C. Leave an opening for stuffing. Sew from D to E.

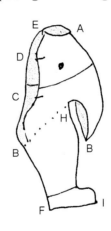
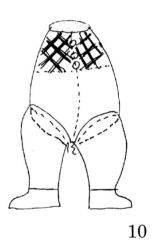

10

Before stuffing, insert pipe cleaners into the bottom legs. This allows the legs to be positioned. Gather neck area on body and attach head. Attach arms, and stuff. Stuff the body and close seams. Refer to the Basic Directions.

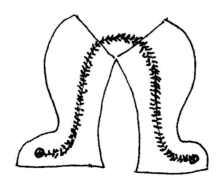

11

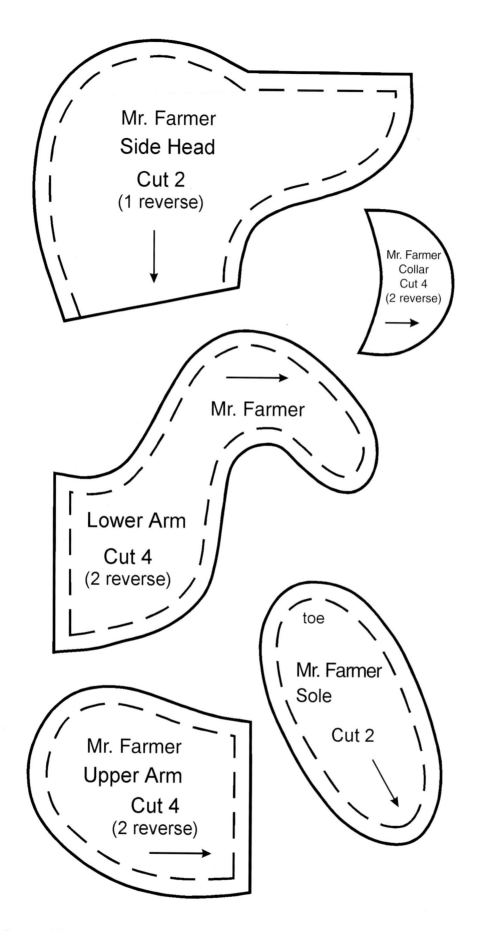

Mr. Farmer
Side Head
Cut 2
(1 reverse)

Mr. Farmer
Collar
Cut 4
(2 reverse)

Mr. Farmer

Lower Arm
Cut 4
(2 reverse)

toe

Mr. Farmer
Sole

Cut 2

Mr. Farmer
Upper Arm
Cut 4
(2 reverse)

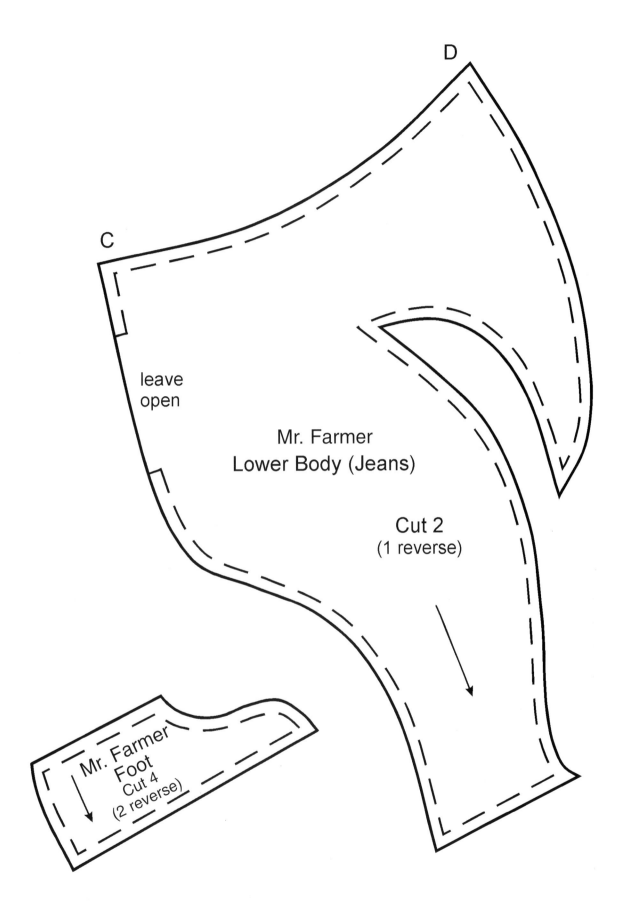

D

C

leave
open

Mr. Farmer
Lower Body (Jeans)

Cut 2
(1 reverse)

Mr. Farmer
Foot
Cut 4
(2 reverse)

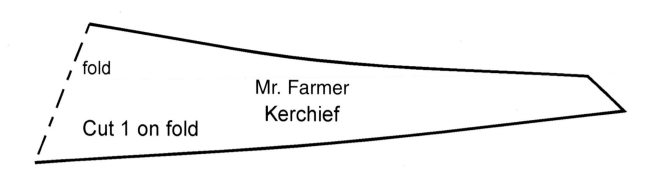

fold

Mr. Farmer
Kerchief

Cut 1 on fold

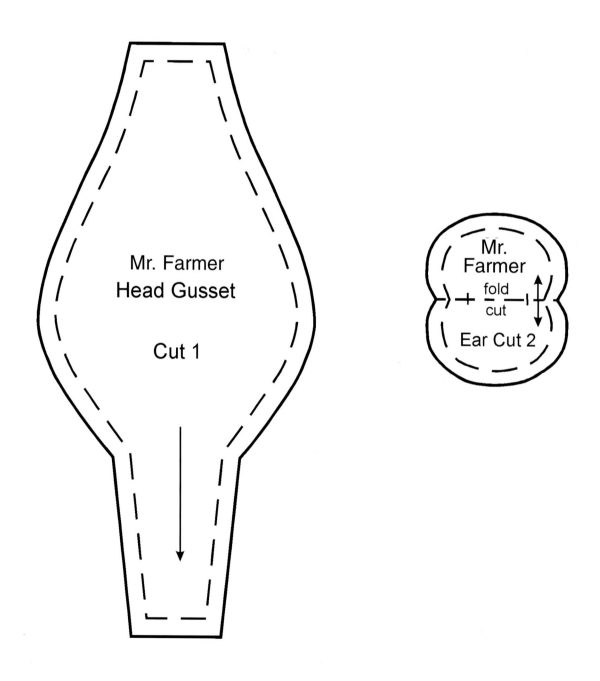

Mr. Farmer
Head Gusset

Cut 1

Mr.
Farmer

fold
cut

Ear Cut 2

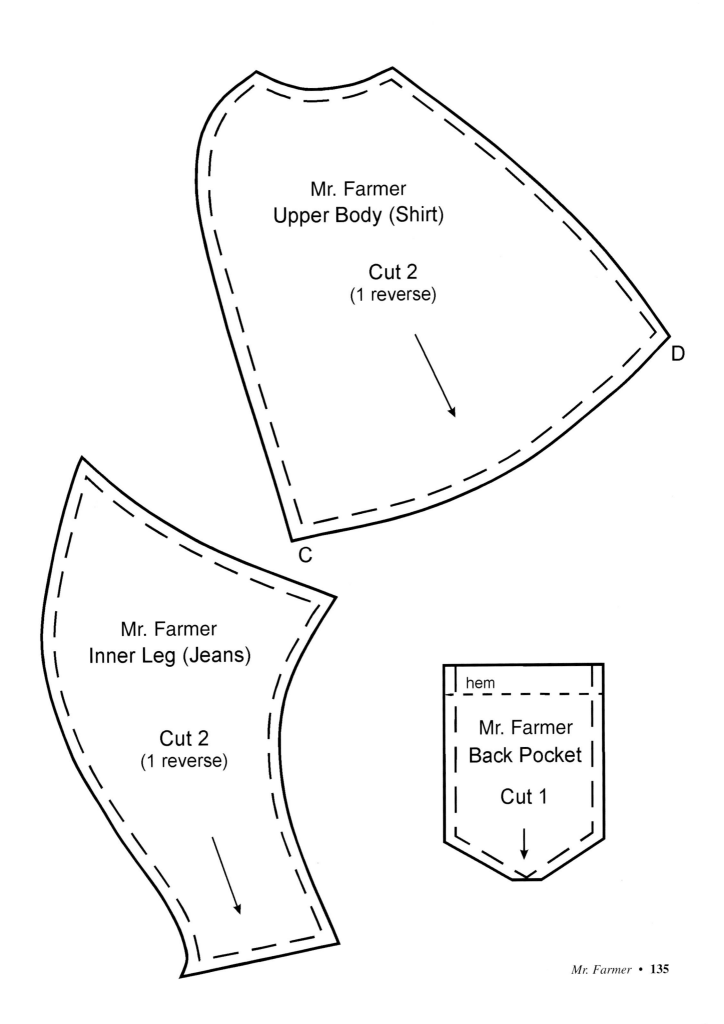

Mr. Farmer
Upper Body (Shirt)

Cut 2
(1 reverse)

D

C

Mr. Farmer
Inner Leg (Jeans)

Cut 2
(1 reverse)

hem

Mr. Farmer
Back Pocket

Cut 1

Mrs. Farmer

(Size: 14 inches; Difficulty Level: 13)

MATERIALS

- ☐ 1/4 yard flower-print upholstery fabric for body suit
- ☐ 1/4 yard light-brown upholstery fabric for legs, arms, chest, soles, head
- ☐ One piece 9" x 30" blue upholstery fabric for skirt
- ☐ One vintage crocheted doily for a shawl
- ☐ 1½ yards 1/4" lace to trim the neck and sleeves
- ☐ One straw hat, circumference approximately 2"
- ☐ One pair 7mm glass or plastic eyes
- ☐ Three T-cotter pin joint sets
- ☐ #5 black pearl cotton for nose and mouth
- ☐ Small piece of beeswax for waxing the nose
- ☐ Sewing-machine thread for seams, color to match fabric
- ☐ Waxed thread for attaching eyes
- ☐ Nylon upholstery thread for closing seams
- ☐ Polyester fiberfill for stuffing

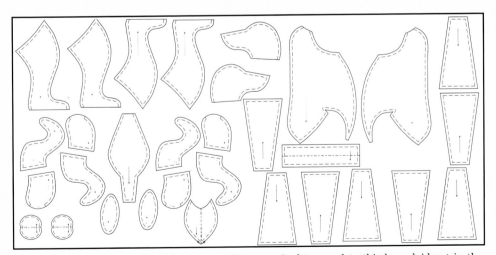

This diagram represents all of the pattern pieces required to complete this bear, laid out in the straight of the fabric. More than one piece of fabric may be required for laying out the pattern pieces.

INSTRUCTIONS

1

Sew two side heads to the center head gusset.

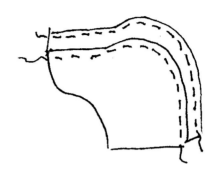

2

Fold center gusset and stitch from the center nose down to the neck edge.

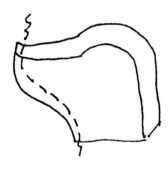

3

Fold ear in half and sew. Cut center section in order to turn the ear.

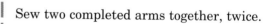

cut and
leave open

4

Sew upper arm (flowered fabric) to lower arm (brown fabric).

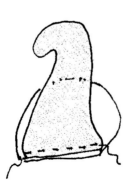

5

Sew two completed arms together, twice.

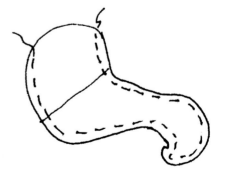

6

Sew upper center front body from A to B.

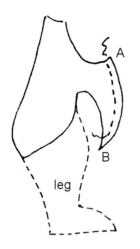

Sew chest to upper body from E to A to E.

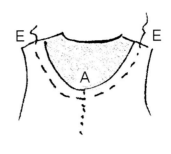

7

8

Sew each leg to upper body.

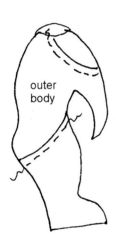

Sew inner leg to leg already on body, from B to F in back, and in the front from H to I.

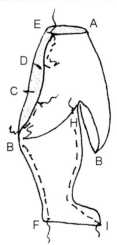

9

10

Sew front body to inner legs along crotch. Point B on the body will match the back-leg seam. Sew from B to C. Leave opening from C to D for stuffing. Sew from D to E.

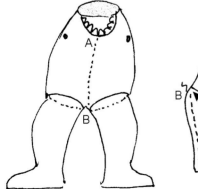
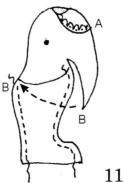

11

Baste the sole into the bottom of each leg, then machine-sew the sole to the leg.

12

Finish the head before attaching it to the body. Refer to the Basic Directions. The corner of the ear nearest the top of the head is placed about 1/4" inside the head gusset at about center top (by eyeball). The other corner is directly down the side head about 1". Make allowance to arch the ear. When stuffing the legs, insert a padded wire into the legs. This allows the legs to bend inward. Curl the ends of the wire to avoid sharp ends.

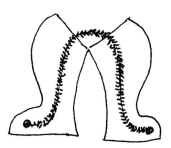 

13

Sew the eight sections of the skirt together. Leave a 2" opening in the last seam for closure.

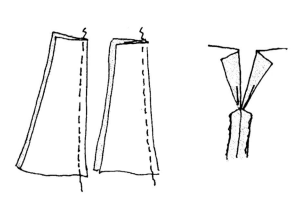

14

Sew a placket to the opening of the skirt.

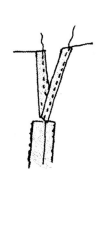

15

Sew the waistband to the skirt.

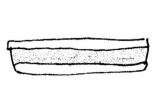 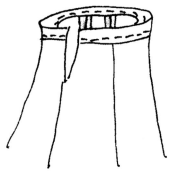

16

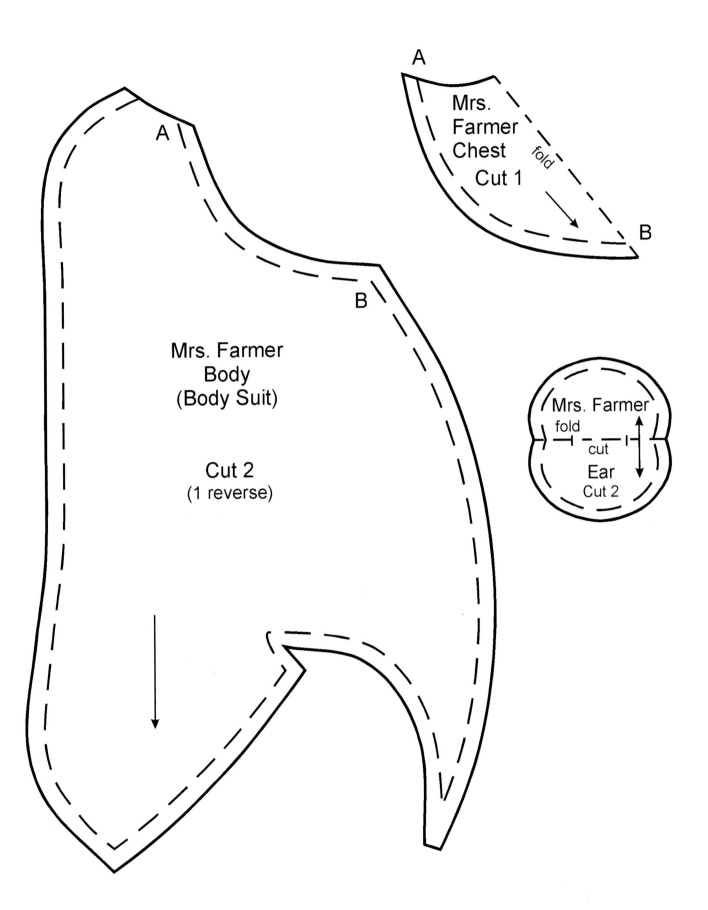

A

Mrs.
Farmer
Chest
Cut 1

fold

B

Mrs. Farmer
Body
(Body Suit)

Cut 2
(1 reverse)

A

B

Mrs. Farmer
fold
cut
Ear
Cut 2

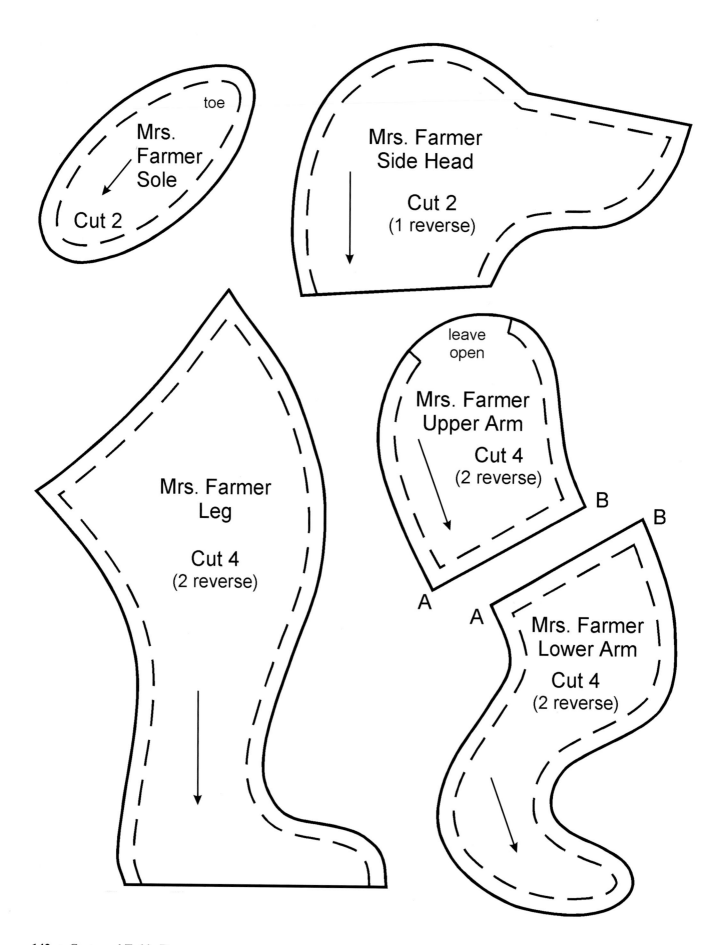

Mrs. Farmer Sole

toe

Cut 2

Mrs. Farmer Side Head

Cut 2
(1 reverse)

leave open

Mrs. Farmer Upper Arm

Cut 4
(2 reverse)

B

A

B

A

Mrs. Farmer Leg

Cut 4
(2 reverse)

Mrs. Farmer Lower Arm

Cut 4
(2 reverse)

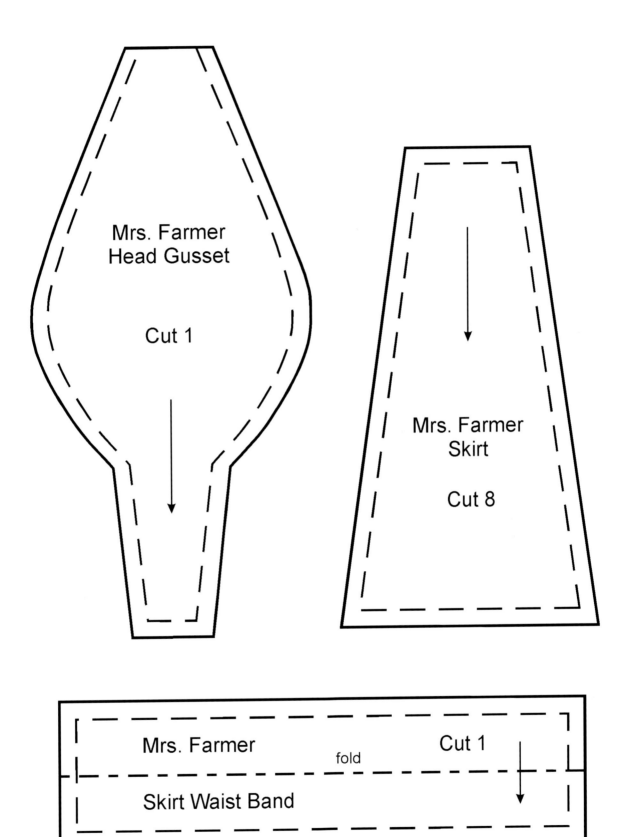

Mrs. Farmer
Head Gusset

Cut 1

Mrs. Farmer
Skirt

Cut 8

Mrs. Farmer
Skirt Waist Band

fold

Cut 1

Sources

SUPPLIES

Bear Street — Dale Junker
415 W. Foothill Blvd., Suite 323
Claremont, CA 91711
909-625-2995

Central Shippee, Inc.
46 Star Lake Road
Bloomingdale, NJ 07403-0135
800-631-8968
www.centralshippee.com
100% wool felt

Edinburgh Imports, Inc.
PO Box 340
Newbury Park, CA 91319-0340
805-376-1700
Fax: 805-376-1711
www.edinburgh.com

Golden Fun Kits
PO Box 10697 Edgemont Branch
Golden, CO 80401-0600
Mail order only

Haida Supplies
29533 Canvasback Dr.
Easton, MD 21601
888-271-0731
www.haidasupplies.com

Intercal Trading Group
1760 Monrovia Avenue, Suite A-17
Costa Mesa, CA 92627
949-645-9396
Fax: 949 645-5471
www.intercaltg.com

Monterey Mills
PO Box 271
Janesville, WI 53547
608-754-2866
Fax: 608-754-3750
Fake fur, stuffing; minimum order $100.

The Leather Factory
800-984-7147
Call for catalog
www.leatherfactory.com

PATTERNS

Celia's Teddies
1562 San Joaquin Ave.
San Jose, CA 95118-1061
408-266-8129
Fax: 408-978-2888
www.celiasteddies.com
celiasteds@aol.com

Purely Neysa
Neysa A. Phillippi
45 Gorman Ave.
Indiana, PA 15701-2244
724-349-1225
Fax: 724-349-3903
purelyneysa@yourinter.net

Robert Zacher Originals
416 E. Broadway
Waukesha, WI 53186
262-544-4739
Fax: 262-544-6676